# The Mysteries of Satanic Rituals and Forbidden Rites

Landon Cross

# Table of Contents

Origins of Darkness..........................................................................4

The dawn of civilization and the emergence of early religious practices ...................................................................................7

Introduction to Satanism..................................................................9

    Defining Satanism: Historical Context and Modern Interpretations ........................................................................................11

    Overview of Contemporary Satanic Movements: LaVeyan Satanism, The Satanic Temple, and Beyond..................................13

The Philosophy of Satanic Rituals....................................................16

    Understanding Satanic Values: Individualism, Rationalism, and Personal Empowerment.............................................................20

    The Role of Rituals in Satanic Practice: Symbolism, Empowerment, and Self-Actualization..............................................................23

Rituals for Personal Empowerment .................................................27

    Rituals to Affirm Individuality, Strength, and Self-Fulfillment.......30

    Techniques for Harnessing Personal Power and Overcoming Obstacles ................................................................................32

Rituals of Symbolism and Self-Reflection .........................................36

    Exploring Symbolic Acts and Gestures in Satanic Rituals .............38

    Rituals for Self-Reflection, Introspection, and Personal Growth...41

Ceremonies for Commemoration ....................................................45

    Marking Life Events from a Satanic Perspective: Births, Weddings, Funerals, and Beyond................................................................48

    Rituals to Honor Milestones and Celebrate Personal Achievements ................................................................................................50

Group Gatherings and Community Building......................................54

The Importance of Community in Satanic Practice ...................... 57

Rituals for Group Bonding, Discussion, and Support ..................... 60

Satanic Holidays and Observances ................................................... 63

Exploring Significant Dates and Events in Satanic History ............ 66

Rituals and Traditions for Observing Satanic Holidays and Festivals ............................................................................................................ 69

Destruction and Symbolic Rebirth ..................................................... 72

Understanding Destruction Rituals in Satanic Practice ................. 75

Rituals for Symbolic Rebirth, Transformation, and Renewal ......... 77

Protection and Empowerment ............................................................ 81

Rituals for Personal Protection, Empowerment, and Defense ...... 84

Techniques for Warding Off Negative Influences and Energies .... 87

Advocacy, Activism, and Social Change ............................................ 91

The Role of Rituals in Promoting Satanic Values and Challenging Social Norms .......................................................................................... 94

Satanic Rituals for Advocacy, Activism, and Fighting Injustice ...... 97

Ethics, Respect, and Non-Violence ................................................... 100

The Ethical Framework of Contemporary Satanism .................... 103

Emphasizing Respect for Others and Non-Violence in Satanic Practice ................................................................................................ 105

Reflecting on the Diversity and Complexity of Satanic Rituals and Practices ............................................................................................... 109

Looking Ahead: The Future of Satanism in a Changing World ........ 112

Satanists have an equivalent to the 10 commandments. ............... 116

Epilogue ................................................................................................ 120

## Origins of Darkness

In the beginning, there was darkness. Not the absence of light, but a primal force, a cosmic void from which all creation emerged. This darkness held within it the seeds of existence, the potential for both light and shadow, for order and chaos. In the ancient mythologies of civilizations long gone, this primordial darkness was revered as the womb of creation, the source from which gods and demons alike were born.

The origins of Satanic rituals can be traced back to these ancient beliefs, to the primal urge to worship and appease the forces of nature, both benevolent and malevolent. In the fertile crescent of Mesopotamia, amidst the ruins of ancient cities like Babylon and Sumer, archaeologists have uncovered evidence of ritualistic practices dating back thousands of years. These early rituals were steeped in animistic beliefs, with gods and spirits inhabiting every aspect of the natural world.

One of the earliest recorded instances of ritualistic worship can be found in the Epic of Gilgamesh, an ancient Mesopotamian poem that dates back to the third millennium BCE. In this epic tale, the hero Gilgamesh ventures into the depths of the underworld in search of immortality, encountering gods, demons, and other supernatural beings along the way. The rituals described in the Epic of Gilgamesh offer a glimpse into the religious practices of ancient Mesopotamia, where offerings were made to appease the gods and ensure a bountiful harvest.

As civilization spread across the ancient world, so too did the practice of ritualistic worship. In ancient Egypt, the pharaohs were revered as gods incarnate, their every action imbued with religious significance. The pyramids, those towering monuments to human ambition, were not just tombs for the dead, but gateways to the afterlife, where the souls of the departed could journey to be reunited with the gods.

In ancient Greece, the pantheon of gods and goddesses ruled over every aspect of mortal life, from the harvest to the hunt, from love to war. The rituals of the Greeks were elaborate affairs, with sacrifices offered to the gods in exchange for their favor. Temples were erected in honor of the gods, where priests and priestesses performed sacred rites to ensure the prosperity and protection of the community.

But it was in ancient Rome that the practice of ritualistic worship reached its zenith. The Roman Empire, with its vast armies and sprawling territories, was a melting pot of cultures and beliefs, where gods from distant lands were welcomed with open arms. The cult of Mithras, with its secretive rituals and initiation ceremonies, spread like wildfire throughout the empire, attracting soldiers and statesmen alike with promises of salvation and immortality.

Yet amidst the grandeur and splendor of ancient civilizations, there lurked a darker side to ritualistic worship. The worship of Baal and Moloch in the ancient Near East involved gruesome sacrifices, with children offered up as burnt offerings to appease the gods. In ancient Carthage, the practice of child sacrifice was widespread, with infants placed in the arms of bronze statues and roasted alive as offerings to the gods.

These ancient rituals, with their blood-soaked altars and whispered incantations, laid the groundwork for the emergence of darker, more esoteric practices in the centuries to come. As the Roman Empire crumbled and the light of civilization dimmed, so too did the ancient gods fade into obscurity, their temples and altars abandoned to the ravages of time.

But the seeds of darkness had been planted, and in the shadows of crumbling temples and forgotten gods, new rituals began to take shape. In the next chapter, we will explore the clandestine gatherings of medieval secret societies, where heretical beliefs and forbidden knowledge flourished amidst the chaos and uncertainty of the Dark Ages.

## The dawn of civilization and the emergence of early religious practices

The dawn of civilization marked a pivotal moment in human history, signaling the transition from nomadic hunter-gatherer societies to settled agricultural communities. This shift brought about profound changes in human social organization, technology, and culture, laying the foundation for the emergence of early religious practices.

As humans settled in fertile river valleys such as the Tigris-Euphrates, Nile, Indus, and Yellow River, they developed complex societies with specialized labor, surplus food production, and hierarchical structures. Within these early civilizations, religious beliefs and rituals played a central role in shaping community cohesion, providing explanations for natural phenomena, and establishing codes of behavior.

The earliest evidence of religious practices dates back to the Paleolithic era, with cave paintings, burial sites, and artifacts suggesting a belief in supernatural forces and rituals to appease or communicate with these unseen powers. Over time, as societies became more complex, religious practices evolved into organized systems of belief with priesthoods, temples, and elaborate rituals to honor gods and goddesses associated with nature, fertility, and the divine order of the cosmos.

In Mesopotamia, the birthplace of civilization, city-states such as Sumer, Akkad, and Babylon developed intricate pantheons of deities, each governing specific aspects of human existence and the natural world. Similarly, in ancient Egypt, the worship of gods like Ra, Osiris, and Isis formed the cornerstone of society, with temples serving as centers of religious activity and political power. The emergence of writing systems such as cuneiform, hieroglyphics, and proto-Elamite enabled the recording of religious texts, myths, and rituals, preserving these beliefs for future generations. Across the ancient world, from the Indus Valley to Mesoamerica, early religious practices reflected the human quest for meaning, identity, and connection to the divine, laying the groundwork for the rich tapestry of religious traditions that would shape the course of history.

# Introduction to Satanism

Satanism is a multifaceted and often misunderstood belief system that has captivated the curiosity and imagination of individuals throughout history. In this introductory chapter, we delve into the rich tapestry of Satanism, exploring its historical roots, diverse interpretations, and modern manifestations.

## Defining Satanism: Historical Context and Modern Interpretations

Satanism, in its broadest sense, encompasses a variety of beliefs, practices, and ideologies centered around the figure of Satan. While the term "Satanism" often conjures images of malevolent rituals and diabolical worship, the reality is far more nuanced. Historically, Satanism has been intertwined with Christian theology, serving as a foil to the concept of God and representing rebellion against religious authority. In modern times, Satanism has evolved into a complex and diverse movement, with different groups and individuals embracing varying interpretations of Satanic philosophy.

**Overview of Contemporary Satanic Movements: LaVeyan Satanism, The Satanic Temple, and Beyond**

Contemporary Satanism is characterized by a plurality of perspectives, each offering unique insights into the nature of Satan and the human condition. One of the most well-known branches of modern Satanism is LaVeyan Satanism, founded by Anton LaVey in the 1960s. LaVeyan Satanism emphasizes individualism, self-indulgence, and rational self-interest, rejecting notions of supernaturalism and embracing a philosophy of "self-as-deity." Another prominent organization is The Satanic Temple, which advocates for the separation of church and state, social justice, and individual autonomy. Beyond these two main movements, there exist numerous other Satanic groups and individuals with their own interpretations and practices, contributing to the rich tapestry of contemporary Satanism.

Through this exploration of Satanism's historical evolution and modern incarnations, we gain a deeper understanding of the diversity, complexity, and enduring appeal of this enigmatic belief system. As we journey further into the rituals, philosophies, and cultural impact of Satanism, we are invited to challenge preconceived notions and explore the deeper truths that lie beneath the surface.

# Defining Satanism: Historical Context and Modern Interpretations

To understand Satanism in its various forms, it is essential to delve into its historical roots and explore the diverse interpretations that have emerged over time. In this chapter, we embark on a journey through history to uncover the origins of Satanism and examine how it has evolved into the multifaceted belief system we encounter today.

**Historical Origins of Satanism:**

The concept of Satanism can be traced back to ancient religious traditions, where figures resembling Satan served as symbols of rebellion, chaos, and opposition to established authority. In early Judeo-Christian theology, Satan (Hebrew: שָׂטָן, meaning "adversary" or "accuser") was depicted as a fallen angel who rebelled against God and tempted humanity into sin. Over time, Satan became associated with various cultural archetypes, including the rebellious hero, the trickster figure, and the embodiment of evil. In medieval Christian Europe, the fear of Satan and demonic forces reached its zenith during periods of religious fervor and social upheaval, leading to the persecution of individuals accused of witchcraft and heresy.

**Modern Interpretations of Satanism:**

In the modern era, Satanism has undergone a profound transformation, evolving into a diverse and decentralized movement with a wide range of interpretations and practices. One of the most influential figures in modern Satanism is Anton

LaVey, who founded the Church of Satan in 1966 and authored The Satanic Bible. LaVeyan Satanism emphasizes individualism, self-indulgence, and the pursuit of personal gratification, rejecting traditional notions of morality and spirituality in favor of rational self-interest. Another prominent organization is The Satanic Temple, founded in 2013, which advocates for secularism, social justice, and the separation of church and state. The Satanic Temple uses Satanic imagery and symbolism to challenge religious privilege and promote pluralism and equality.

**Varieties of Satanic Belief:**

Beyond LaVeyan Satanism and The Satanic Temple, there exist numerous other Satanic groups, organizations, and individuals with their own interpretations and practices. Some practitioners of modern Satanism embrace a more mystical or occult approach, drawing inspiration from esoteric traditions, ceremonial magic, and ancient mythology. Others adopt a more atheistic or humanistic perspective, viewing Satan as a symbol of individualism, rebellion, and intellectual freedom. Regardless of their specific beliefs and practices, contemporary Satanists share a common rejection of dogma, authority, and religious conformity, choosing instead to embrace personal autonomy, critical thinking, and rational inquiry.

The history and diversity of Satanism reveal a complex and multifaceted belief system that defies easy categorization or definition. From its ancient origins as a symbol of rebellion to its modern incarnations as a philosophical and cultural movement, Satanism continues to evolve and adapt to changing social, cultural, and political contexts. By exploring the historical context and modern interpretations of Satanism, we gain a deeper appreciation for the richness and complexity of this enigmatic belief system and the individuals who embrace it.

## Overview of Contemporary Satanic Movements: LaVeyan Satanism, The Satanic Temple, and Beyond

Contemporary Satanism encompasses a diverse array of movements, ideologies, and organizations, each with its own unique interpretations of Satanic philosophy and practice. In this chapter, we explore some of the most prominent contemporary Satanic movements, including LaVeyan Satanism, The Satanic Temple, and other emerging groups that represent the expanding landscape of Satanic thought and expression.

**LaVeyan Satanism:**

Founded by Anton Szandor LaVey in 1966 with the establishment of the Church of Satan, LaVeyan Satanism represents one of the most well-known and influential branches of contemporary Satanism. LaVeyan Satanism is characterized by its emphasis on individualism, rational self-interest, and the pursuit of personal gratification. Central to LaVeyan philosophy is the concept of the "Satanic" as a symbol of human nature, embodying qualities such as pride, independence, and self-determination. The Satanic Bible, written by LaVey, serves as a foundational text for LaVeyan Satanists, outlining key principles and rituals for living a Satanic lifestyle. LaVeyan Satanism rejects supernatural beliefs and deities, instead focusing on the power of the individual to shape their own destiny and find meaning in life on their own terms.

**The Satanic Temple:**

Founded in 2013 by Lucien Greaves and Malcolm Jarry, The Satanic Temple (TST) has quickly emerged as a prominent voice for secularism, social justice, and religious pluralism. Unlike LaVeyan Satanism, which emphasizes atheism and individualism, TST views Satan as a metaphorical symbol of rebellion against tyranny, injustice, and oppression. TST advocates for the separation of church and state, promotes scientific literacy and rational inquiry, and challenges religious privilege and discrimination through activism and advocacy. The organization's campaigns and public demonstrations, often featuring Satanic imagery and rituals, have garnered widespread media attention and sparked public debate about the role of religion in society.

**Beyond LaVeyan Satanism and The Satanic Temple:**

In addition to LaVeyan Satanism and The Satanic Temple, there exist numerous other Satanic groups, organizations, and individuals with their own interpretations and practices. Some practitioners of modern Satanism embrace a more mystical or occult approach, drawing inspiration from esoteric traditions, ceremonial magic, and ancient mythology. Others adopt a more atheistic or humanistic perspective, viewing Satan as a symbol of individualism, rebellion, and intellectual freedom. Emerging Satanic groups and movements continue to challenge traditional notions of religion, morality, and spirituality, pushing the boundaries of Satanic thought and practice in new and innovative ways.

The contemporary Satanic landscape is diverse, dynamic, and ever-evolving, reflecting the complexity of human nature and the ongoing search for meaning and purpose in a secular world. LaVeyan Satanism, The Satanic Temple, and other Satanic movements each offer unique perspectives on Satanic philosophy and practice, providing individuals with opportunities for self-discovery, empowerment, and social engagement. By exploring the various facets of contemporary Satanism, we gain insight into the diversity and richness of Satanic thought and its relevance to modern society.

## The Philosophy of Satanic Rituals

Satanic rituals serve as integral components of Satanic practice, embodying the philosophical principles, symbolic imagery, and transformative potential inherent in Satanism. In this chapter, we delve deep into the philosophy of Satanic rituals, exploring their origins, meanings, and practical applications within contemporary Satanism. Through an extensive examination of Satanic ritual practices, we aim to unravel the complex layers of symbolism, psychology, and empowerment that underlie these rituals, shedding light on their profound significance for practitioners of Satanism.

**Origins of Satanic Rituals:**

The origins of Satanic rituals can be traced back to ancient religious traditions, where ritualistic practices served as means of communing with divine forces, affirming social bonds, and expressing cultural identity. In pre-Christian pagan societies, rituals involving sacrifices, invocations, and symbolic gestures were common ways of honoring deities, appeasing spirits, and ensuring the prosperity of the community. With the rise of Christianity and the demonization of pagan beliefs, many of these ritual practices were suppressed or co-opted into Christian forms of worship, resulting in the demonization of pagan gods and the vilification of ritualistic practices associated with them.

In the modern era, Satanic rituals experienced a resurgence with the emergence of contemporary Satanic movements such as LaVeyan Satanism and The Satanic Temple. Anton LaVey, founder of the Church of Satan, introduced a system of rituals based on principles of psychodrama, symbolism, and personal empowerment. LaVey's rituals drew inspiration from diverse sources, including Western occultism, psychological theory, and theatrical performance, creating a unique blend of ceremonial practices designed to evoke emotional responses and catalyze personal transformation. Similarly, The Satanic Temple developed its own rituals and ceremonies, often employing Satanic imagery and symbolism to challenge religious norms, advocate for social justice, and promote individual autonomy.

**The Philosophy of Satanic Rituals:**

At the heart of Satanic rituals lies a philosophy rooted in individualism, rationalism, and personal empowerment. Unlike traditional religious rituals, which often involve acts of worship, supplication, or submission to divine authority, Satanic rituals are designed to celebrate human agency, assert personal autonomy, and affirm Satanic values. Satanic rituals serve as symbolic enactments of Satanic philosophy, embodying the principles of self-actualization, defiance, and rebellion against oppressive forces.

One of the key principles underlying Satanic rituals is the concept of psychodrama, a technique borrowed from psychology and theater that involves the enactment of symbolic narratives to evoke emotional responses and facilitate personal transformation. In Satanic rituals, participants are encouraged to engage in role-playing, visualization, and sensory stimulation to immerse themselves in the ritual experience and tap into their subconscious minds. Through the use of ritualized gestures, words, and actions, Satanic rituals create a sense of catharsis, allowing participants to release pent-up emotions, confront inner demons, and embrace their true selves.

Another important aspect of Satanic rituals is their emphasis on symbolism and metaphor. Satanic rituals make extensive use of symbols, imagery, and archetypes drawn from mythology, folklore, and occult tradition to convey deeper meanings and stimulate the imagination. Symbols such as the pentagram, the inverted cross, and the Baphomet are commonly used in Satanic rituals to represent concepts such as individualism, rebellion, and spiritual enlightenment. By engaging with these symbols in ritual contexts, participants are able to explore their own interpretations and forge personal connections to Satanic ideology.

**Practical Applications of Satanic Rituals:**

In addition to their symbolic and psychological significance, Satanic rituals also serve practical purposes within contemporary Satanic practice. Satanic rituals can be used as tools for personal empowerment, helping individuals to overcome fears, break free from social conditioning, and assert their own desires and ambitions. Through the ritualized affirmation of Satanic values and principles, participants are able to cultivate a sense of self-confidence, self-reliance, and self-respect, enabling them to navigate the challenges of life with clarity and conviction.

Satanic rituals also play a role in fostering community and camaraderie among Satanic practitioners. Group rituals, such as Black Masses, Sabbaths, and other communal ceremonies, provide opportunities for like-minded individuals to come together, share experiences, and strengthen bonds of solidarity. By participating in group rituals, Satanic practitioners are able to draw strength and inspiration from one another, forming networks of support and mutual respect that transcend traditional religious boundaries.

Furthermore, Satanic rituals can be used as a form of social activism and cultural critique. The Satanic Temple, for example, has gained notoriety for its public demonstrations and ritual performances, which often challenge religious privilege, advocate for secularism, and protest against social injustice. Through the use of Satanic imagery and symbolism, The Satanic Temple seeks to provoke thought, spark dialogue, and promote positive social change, highlighting the hypocrisy and irrationality of religious dogma and authoritarianism.

In conclusion, the philosophy of Satanic rituals encompasses a rich tapestry of symbolism, psychology, and empowerment that reflects the core values and beliefs of contemporary Satanism. From their ancient origins as expressions of pagan spirituality to their modern incarnations as tools for personal transformation and social activism, Satanic rituals continue to evolve and adapt to changing cultural contexts. By exploring the philosophy of Satanic rituals, we gain insight into the profound significance of these ceremonial practices for practitioners of Satanism, as well as their broader cultural and philosophical implications for society as a whole.

## Understanding Satanic Values: Individualism, Rationalism, and Personal Empowerment

At the core of Satanism lie a set of values that prioritize individual autonomy, rational inquiry, and personal empowerment. In this chapter, we delve deep into the principles that underpin Satanic philosophy, exploring the significance of individualism, rationalism, and personal empowerment within the context of Satanism. Through an examination of Satanic values, we aim to gain a deeper understanding of the guiding principles that shape Satanic thought and practice, as well as their implications for personal and societal transformation.

**Individualism in Satanism:**

Individualism stands as one of the foundational pillars of Satanic philosophy, emphasizing the sovereignty of the individual and the rejection of external authority or dogma. Satanism places a high value on personal freedom, self-expression, and self-determination, encouraging individuals to think for themselves, pursue their own desires, and chart their own paths in life. Unlike traditional religious ideologies that prioritize obedience, conformity, and submission to divine will, Satanism celebrates the uniqueness and diversity of human experience, recognizing that each individual possesses the power and agency to shape their own destiny.

Central to the concept of individualism in Satanism is the idea of self-actualization, the process by which individuals strive to realize their full potential and achieve fulfillment in life. Satanism encourages individuals to embrace their true selves, pursue their passions, and cultivate their talents and strengths, rather than conforming to societal norms or adhering to arbitrary moral codes. By asserting their individuality and asserting their autonomy, Satanists affirm their inherent worth and dignity as human beings, refusing to be defined or constrained by external expectations or judgments.

**Rationalism in Satanism:**

Rationalism serves as another cornerstone of Satanic philosophy, advocating for critical thinking, skepticism, and empiricism as the primary means of understanding the world and making informed decisions. Satanism rejects supernatural beliefs, superstition, and blind faith in favor of evidence-based reasoning, logical analysis, and scientific inquiry. Satanists value reason and intellect as tools for navigating the complexities of existence, seeking to understand the natural world through observation, experimentation, and rational discourse.

Rationalism in Satanism extends beyond mere skepticism towards religious or supernatural claims; it encompasses a broader commitment to intellectual honesty, intellectual autonomy, and intellectual integrity. Satanists value intellectual curiosity, open-mindedness, and a willingness to question received wisdom and challenge conventional wisdom. By embracing rationalism, Satanists empower themselves to think critically, evaluate evidence, and arrive at reasoned conclusions based on objective reality, rather than relying on subjective beliefs or dogmatic assertions.

**Personal Empowerment in Satanism:**

Personal empowerment represents a central tenet of Satanic philosophy, emphasizing the cultivation of self-confidence, self-reliance, and self-esteem as the keys to personal success and fulfillment. Satanism rejects the notion of original sin or inherent human depravity, instead celebrating the potential for greatness and achievement that lies within each individual. Satanists view adversity as an opportunity for growth, challenge as a catalyst for transformation, and setbacks as stepping stones towards personal excellence.

Empowerment in Satanism is not merely a matter of self-improvement or self-help; it is a radical affirmation of the inherent worth and dignity of every individual, regardless of their background, circumstances, or abilities. Satanists reject victimhood and embrace responsibility, recognizing that they alone are the masters of their own destinies and the architects of their own fates. Through self-empowerment, Satanists reclaim control over their lives, assert their autonomy, and refuse to be passive spectators in the drama of existence.

In conclusion, the values of individualism, rationalism, and personal empowerment lie at the heart of Satanic philosophy, providing a framework for understanding the world, navigating the challenges of life, and pursuing personal excellence. By embracing these values, Satanists affirm their commitment to personal freedom, intellectual honesty, and self-actualization, as well as their rejection of external authority, blind faith, and victimhood. Understanding Satanic values allows us to gain insight into the guiding principles that shape Satanic thought and practice, as well as their broader implications for personal and societal transformation.

# The Role of Rituals in Satanic Practice: Symbolism, Empowerment, and Self-Actualization

Rituals serve as integral components of Satanic practice, providing practitioners with opportunities for self-expression, personal growth, and spiritual exploration. In this chapter, we delve deep into the role of rituals in Satanism, exploring their symbolic significance, empowering potential, and transformative effects on individuals. Through an examination of Satanic rituals, we aim to unravel the complex layers of symbolism, psychology, and empowerment that underlie these ceremonial practices, shedding light on their profound significance for practitioners of Satanism.

**Symbolism in Satanic Rituals:**

Satanic rituals are steeped in symbolism, drawing upon a rich tapestry of mythological, occult, and cultural imagery to convey deeper meanings and evoke emotional responses. Symbols such as the pentagram, the inverted cross, and the sigil of Baphomet serve as potent archetypes in Satanic rituals, representing concepts such as individualism, rebellion, and enlightenment. Through the use of symbolic gestures, words, and actions, Satanic rituals create a sacred space in which participants can explore their own interpretations and forge personal connections to Satanic ideology.

The symbolism of Satanic rituals extends beyond mere aesthetics; it serves as a means of communication, expression, and transformation. By engaging with symbols in ritual contexts, participants are able to tap into their subconscious minds, accessing hidden layers of meaning and unlocking latent potentials within themselves. Satanic rituals invite participants to embody the archetypes represented by symbolic imagery, enabling them to explore different aspects of their own personalities and consciousnesses.

**Empowerment in Satanic Rituals:**

Empowerment represents a central theme in Satanic rituals, emphasizing the cultivation of self-confidence, self-reliance, and self-esteem as the keys to personal growth and fulfillment. Satanic rituals provide practitioners with opportunities to assert their individuality, overcome fears, and break free from social conditioning, empowering them to embrace their true selves and pursue their own desires and ambitions. Through ritualized acts of self-assertion and self-actualization, participants are able to reclaim control over their lives, assert their autonomy, and affirm their inherent worth as human beings.

One of the primary mechanisms through which Satanic rituals empower practitioners is through the experience of catharsis, a process of emotional release and purification that occurs during ritualized activities. By engaging in ritualized gestures, words, and actions, participants are able to express and process pent-up emotions, confront inner demons, and release negative energy, creating space for personal growth and transformation. Satanic rituals provide practitioners with a safe and supportive environment in which to explore their own psyches, confront their fears, and transcend their limitations, enabling them to emerge stronger, more resilient, and more self-assured.

**Self-Actualization in Satanic Rituals:**

Self-actualization serves as the ultimate goal of Satanic rituals, representing the process by which individuals strive to realize their full potential and achieve fulfillment in life. Satanic rituals provide practitioners with tools and techniques for personal transformation, enabling them to overcome obstacles, cultivate their talents, and become the best versions of themselves. Through the practice of Satanic rituals, participants are able to tap into their inner resources, unleash their creative energies, and manifest their dreams and aspirations into reality.

One of the key mechanisms through which Satanic rituals facilitate self-actualization is through the cultivation of mindfulness and presence in the moment. By engaging in ritualized activities with focused intention and attention, participants are able to heighten their awareness of their thoughts, feelings, and sensations, enabling them to gain insight into their own psyche and behavior. Satanic rituals provide practitioners with opportunities for self-reflection, introspection, and self-discovery, allowing them to uncover hidden truths, unlock dormant potentials, and unleash their inner greatness.

In conclusion, the role of rituals in Satanic practice is multifaceted and complex, encompassing aspects of symbolism, empowerment, and self-actualization. Satanic rituals provide practitioners with opportunities to engage with symbolic imagery, express their individuality, and explore their own psyches in a supportive and transformative environment. By embracing the power of rituals, Satanists are able to tap into their inner resources, unlock their hidden potentials, and embark on the journey of self-discovery and personal growth. Through the practice of Satanic rituals, individuals are able to assert their autonomy, assert their individuality, and affirm their inherent worth as human beings, ultimately leading to a deeper sense of fulfillment and purpose in life.

## Rituals for Personal Empowerment

Personal empowerment stands as a central theme in Satanic philosophy, emphasizing the cultivation of self-confidence, self-reliance, and self-esteem as essential components of individual autonomy and fulfillment. In this chapter, we explore the rituals designed specifically to foster personal empowerment within the framework of Satanism. These rituals provide practitioners with tools and techniques to assert their individuality, overcome obstacles, and embrace their inherent potential for greatness. Through an examination of rituals for personal empowerment, we aim to unravel the strategies and practices that enable Satanists to cultivate strength, resilience, and self-assurance in the face of life's challenges.

**Rituals of Self-Affirmation:**

Rituals of self-affirmation serve as foundational practices for personal empowerment in Satanism, providing practitioners with opportunities to assert their identity, values, and aspirations. These rituals often involve affirmations, visualizations, and symbolic gestures designed to reinforce positive beliefs and attitudes about oneself. Through the repetition of affirmations such as "I am strong," "I am capable," and "I am worthy," practitioners are able to cultivate a mindset of self-confidence and self-worth, overcoming self-doubt and negative self-talk. Rituals of self-affirmation empower practitioners to recognize their inherent worth and dignity as human beings, regardless of external judgments or expectations.

**Rituals of Self-Actualization:**

Rituals of self-actualization focus on the realization of one's full potential and the pursuit of personal excellence in all areas of life. These rituals provide practitioners with opportunities to set goals, clarify values, and develop strategies for personal growth and achievement. Through visualization exercises, goal-setting rituals, and action-oriented practices, participants are able to identify their passions, talents, and aspirations, taking concrete steps towards manifesting their dreams into reality. Rituals of self-actualization empower practitioners to overcome obstacles, embrace challenges, and strive for excellence in their endeavors, fostering a sense of fulfillment and purpose in life.

**Rituals of Self-Defense:**

Rituals of self-defense serve as protective practices for personal empowerment, enabling practitioners to assert boundaries, protect their energy, and defend themselves against external threats or negative influences. These rituals often involve visualization techniques, energy work, and symbolic acts of empowerment designed to fortify the practitioner's psychic and emotional defenses. Through the practice of psychic shielding, banishing rituals, and boundary-setting exercises, participants are able to create a sense of safety and security within themselves, guarding against psychic attacks, emotional vampires, and toxic relationships. Rituals of self-defense empower practitioners to assert their autonomy, protect their well-being, and cultivate a sense of inner strength and resilience in the face of adversity.

**Rituals of Self-Transformation:**

Rituals of self-transformation focus on personal growth and evolution, enabling practitioners to release old patterns, embrace new possibilities, and become the best versions of themselves. These rituals often involve acts of catharsis, purification, and renewal designed to facilitate inner transformation and spiritual awakening. Through the practice of ritualized catharsis, participants are able to release pent-up emotions, confront inner demons, and let go of limiting beliefs that hold them back from reaching their full potential. Rituals of self-transformation empower practitioners to embrace change, embrace uncertainty, and embrace the journey of self-discovery and self-mastery.

In conclusion, rituals for personal empowerment represent essential practices within the framework of Satanism, enabling practitioners to assert their individuality, cultivate strength, and pursue personal excellence in all areas of life. Through rituals of self-affirmation, self-actualization, self-defense, and self-transformation, Satanists are able to tap into their inner resources, unlock their hidden potentials, and embark on the journey of self-discovery and personal growth. By embracing the power of rituals, practitioners are able to assert their autonomy, assert their individuality, and affirm their inherent worth as human beings, ultimately leading to a deeper sense of fulfillment and purpose in life.

## Rituals to Affirm Individuality, Strength, and Self-Fulfillment

Satanism places a strong emphasis on individuality, strength, and self-fulfillment, recognizing the inherent value and potential of each individual. In this chapter, we explore rituals specifically designed to affirm these qualities within the framework of Satanic practice. These rituals serve as powerful tools for practitioners to assert their identity, cultivate inner strength, and pursue personal fulfillment in alignment with Satanic values. Through an examination of rituals to affirm individuality, strength, and self-fulfillment, we aim to unravel the strategies and practices that enable Satanists to embrace their true selves and live authentically.

**Rituals of Self-Identification:**

Rituals of self-identification are designed to help practitioners assert their individuality and affirm their unique identity within the context of Satanism. These rituals often involve symbolic acts or gestures that represent the practitioner's personal beliefs, values, and aspirations. For example, participants may create personalized sigils, symbols, or talismans to represent aspects of their identity or goals. Through the practice of ritualized self-identification, practitioners are able to express their individuality, celebrate their differences, and affirm their place within the Satanic community.

**Rituals of Strength:**

Rituals of strength focus on cultivating inner resilience, fortitude, and determination in the face of life's challenges. These rituals provide practitioners with opportunities to tap into their inner resources, overcome obstacles, and embrace their inherent power as individuals. Rituals of strength often involve visualization exercises, affirmation rituals, and physical practices designed to build confidence and self-assurance. For example, participants may engage in rituals that involve lifting weights, performing martial arts, or facing their fears in controlled environments. Through the practice of rituals of strength, practitioners are able to develop a sense of inner strength and resilience, empowering them to navigate life's difficulties with courage and conviction.

**Rituals of Self-Fulfillment:**

Rituals of self-fulfillment are designed to help practitioners pursue their passions, fulfill their potential, and live life to the fullest. These rituals provide opportunities for self-expression, creativity, and personal growth, enabling practitioners to align their actions with their deepest desires and aspirations. Rituals of self-fulfillment often involve goal-setting exercises, visualization techniques, and affirmation rituals designed to clarify values and intentions. For example, participants may create vision boards, write out their goals, or engage in guided meditations to manifest their dreams into reality. Through the practice of rituals of self-fulfillment, practitioners are able to cultivate a sense of purpose and meaning in life, empowering them to pursue their passions and create the life they truly desire.

In conclusion, rituals to affirm individuality, strength, and self-fulfillment represent essential practices within the framework of Satanic philosophy, enabling practitioners to embrace their true selves and live authentically. Through rituals of self-identification, strength, and self-fulfillment, Satanists are able to assert their identity, cultivate inner resilience, and pursue personal fulfillment in alignment with Satanic values. By embracing these rituals, practitioners are able to tap into their inner resources, overcome obstacles, and create the life they truly desire, ultimately leading to a deeper sense of fulfillment and purpose in life.

## Techniques for Harnessing Personal Power and Overcoming Obstacles

In the pursuit of personal empowerment and self-actualization, Satanists employ various techniques to harness their inner strength and overcome obstacles. These techniques draw upon the principles of Satanic philosophy, emphasizing individual autonomy, rationalism, and personal empowerment. In this chapter, we explore the strategies and practices used by Satanists to cultivate personal power and navigate the challenges of life.

Through an examination of techniques for harnessing personal power and overcoming obstacles, we aim to unravel the methods that enable Satanists to assert their autonomy, overcome adversity, and thrive in the face of adversity.

**Mindfulness and Self-Awareness:**

Mindfulness and self-awareness serve as foundational practices for harnessing personal power and overcoming obstacles in Satanism. These practices involve cultivating present-moment awareness and non-judgmental observation of one's thoughts, feelings, and sensations. By developing mindfulness and self-awareness, practitioners are able to gain insight into their own inner workings, identify limiting beliefs and patterns of behavior, and cultivate a greater sense of clarity and self-understanding. Through the practice of mindfulness, Satanists learn to observe their thoughts and emotions without attachment or judgment, enabling them to respond to life's challenges with greater presence, equanimity, and resilience.

**Visualization and Creative Visualization:**

Visualization and creative visualization techniques are powerful tools for harnessing personal power and manifesting desired outcomes in Satanism. These techniques involve the use of mental imagery, imagination, and visualization to create a clear and vivid picture of one's goals, desires, and intentions. By visualizing desired outcomes in detail, practitioners are able to align their thoughts, emotions, and actions with their goals, thereby increasing the likelihood of success and fulfillment. Creative visualization techniques often involve the use of affirmations, positive imagery, and sensory visualization to evoke the desired emotional state and reinforce positive beliefs about oneself and one's abilities.

**Affirmations and Positive Affirmations:**

Affirmations and positive affirmations are another effective technique for harnessing personal power and overcoming obstacles in Satanism. Affirmations are positive statements or declarations that affirm desired outcomes, qualities, or beliefs about oneself. By repeating affirmations regularly, practitioners are able to reprogram their subconscious minds, replace negative self-talk with positive self-affirmations, and cultivate a mindset of self-confidence and self-belief. Positive affirmations can be tailored to specific goals or areas of focus, such as health, wealth, relationships, or personal development, and can be used in conjunction with other techniques such as visualization and meditation to amplify their effectiveness.

**Meditation and Mindfulness Practices:**

Meditation and mindfulness practices are integral components of Satanic philosophy, providing practitioners with tools to cultivate inner peace, clarity, and resilience in the face of life's challenges. These practices involve the cultivation of present-moment awareness, concentration, and equanimity through the practice of focused attention or open awareness meditation. By training the mind to remain centered and focused, practitioners are able to develop greater emotional regulation, cognitive flexibility, and stress resilience, enabling them to navigate difficult situations with greater ease and grace. Meditation and mindfulness practices also provide opportunities for self-reflection, introspection, and insight, allowing practitioners to gain deeper understanding of themselves and their place in the world.

In conclusion, techniques for harnessing personal power and overcoming obstacles are essential practices within the framework of Satanic philosophy, enabling practitioners to assert their autonomy, cultivate resilience, and thrive in the face of adversity. Through the practice of mindfulness, visualization, affirmations, and meditation, Satanists are able to harness their inner resources, overcome limiting beliefs, and create the life they truly desire. By embracing these techniques, practitioners are able to cultivate a greater sense of self-confidence, clarity, and purpose, ultimately leading to a deeper sense of fulfillment and empowerment in life.

## Rituals of Symbolism and Self-Reflection

Rituals of symbolism and self-reflection are integral to Satanic practice, providing practitioners with opportunities to explore deeper layers of meaning, confront inner truths, and cultivate self-awareness. In this chapter, we delve into the significance of rituals centered around symbolism and self-reflection within the framework of Satanism. These rituals serve as powerful tools for personal growth, empowerment, and spiritual development. Through an exploration of rituals of symbolism and self-reflection, we aim to unravel the methods and practices that enable Satanists to gain insight into themselves and the world around them.

**Symbolism in Satanic Rituals:**

Symbolism plays a crucial role in Satanic rituals, serving as a language of the subconscious mind and a gateway to deeper understanding. Satanic rituals often incorporate symbolic imagery, gestures, and actions to convey abstract concepts and evoke emotional responses. Symbols such as the pentagram, the inverted cross, and the sigil of Baphomet hold potent meanings within Satanic philosophy, representing themes of individualism, rebellion, and enlightenment. By engaging with symbolic elements in ritual contexts, practitioners are able to tap into their subconscious minds, accessing hidden truths and unlocking deeper levels of awareness.

Rituals of symbolism often involve the use of ritualized gestures, words, and actions to evoke specific states of consciousness or emotional responses. For example, participants may perform gestures such as the Sign of the Horns or recite incantations to invoke feelings of strength, empowerment, or defiance. Through the practice of rituals of symbolism, practitioners are able to connect with archetypal energies, embody mythical narratives, and explore their own inner landscapes in a safe and supportive environment.

**Self-Reflection in Satanic Rituals:**

Self-reflection is a central practice in Satanic philosophy, providing practitioners with opportunities to examine their beliefs, values, and behaviors with honesty and clarity. Satanic rituals often incorporate elements of self-reflection, inviting participants to engage in introspection, contemplation, and self-examination. These rituals may involve guided meditation, journaling exercises, or group discussions focused on exploring personal experiences, insights, and challenges.

Rituals of self-reflection encourage practitioners to confront their fears, doubts, and insecurities, and to embrace their strengths, passions, and aspirations. By engaging in practices of self-reflection, practitioners are able to gain insight into their own motivations, patterns of behavior, and underlying beliefs, enabling them to make informed choices and take deliberate action towards personal growth and fulfillment. Self-reflection rituals also provide opportunities for practitioners to connect with others, share experiences, and receive support and feedback from like-minded individuals on their journey of self-discovery.

In conclusion, rituals of symbolism and self-reflection are essential practices within the framework of Satanic philosophy, providing practitioners with tools for exploring deeper layers of meaning, confronting inner truths, and cultivating self-awareness. Through rituals of symbolism, practitioners are able to connect with archetypal energies and tap into their subconscious minds, unlocking hidden potentials and gaining insight into themselves and the world around them. Similarly, rituals of self-reflection enable practitioners to examine their beliefs, values, and behaviors with honesty and clarity, empowering them to make conscious choices and take deliberate action towards personal growth and fulfillment. By embracing these rituals, Satanists are able to navigate the complexities of existence with greater understanding, resilience, and authenticity, ultimately leading to a deeper sense of empowerment and purpose in life.

## Exploring Symbolic Acts and Gestures in Satanic Rituals

Symbolic acts and gestures hold profound significance within Satanic rituals, serving as potent tools for communication, expression, and transformation. In this chapter, we delve into the exploration of symbolic acts and gestures in Satanic rituals, examining their meanings, purposes, and effects on practitioners. These rituals play a crucial role in facilitating personal empowerment, self-expression, and spiritual evolution within the framework of Satanism. Through an in-depth exploration of symbolic acts and gestures, we aim to unravel the rich tapestry of symbolism and meaning that underlies Satanic ritual practice.

**The Power of Symbolism in Satanic Rituals:**

Symbolism lies at the heart of Satanic rituals, providing practitioners with a language through which to communicate complex ideas, emotions, and experiences. Satanic rituals often incorporate symbolic imagery, gestures, and actions to evoke specific states of consciousness or to convey abstract concepts. Symbols such as the pentagram, the inverted cross, and the sigil of Baphomet hold potent meanings within Satanic philosophy, representing themes of individualism, rebellion, and enlightenment.

# Symbolic acts and gestures in Satanic rituals serve multiple purposes, including:

**Invocation of Archetypal Energies:** Symbolic acts and gestures are used to invoke archetypal energies and evoke specific emotional responses or states of consciousness. For example, the Sign of the Horns gesture may be used to invoke feelings of strength, power, and defiance, while the act of tracing the pentagram may be used to invoke protection, balance, and spiritual insight.

**Personal Empowerment:** Symbolic acts and gestures are used to empower practitioners and reinforce positive beliefs and attitudes about themselves. By engaging in ritualized acts of self-assertion, practitioners are able to cultivate a sense of confidence, self-reliance, and self-worth, overcoming self-doubt and negative self-talk.

**Transformation and Catharsis:** Symbolic acts and gestures are used to facilitate personal transformation and emotional catharsis. Through the practice of ritualized gestures, words, and actions, practitioners are able to release pent-up emotions, confront inner demons, and let go of limiting beliefs that hold them back from reaching their full potential.

## Examples of Symbolic Acts and Gestures in Satanic Rituals:

**The Sign of the Horns:** The Sign of the Horns gesture, made by extending the index and pinky fingers while holding the middle and ring fingers down with the thumb, is a widely recognized symbol of defiance, strength, and rebellion within Satanic culture. This gesture is often used in Satanic rituals to invoke feelings of empowerment and assertiveness, as well as to ward off negative energies or influences.

**The Inverted Cross:** The inverted cross is a powerful symbol of defiance and opposition to religious authority within Satanic philosophy. In Satanic rituals, the inverted cross may be used to symbolize the rejection of traditional religious norms and the embrace of individual autonomy and freedom of thought.

**The Tracing of the Pentagram:** The pentagram is a sacred symbol in Satanic philosophy, representing the balance of elemental forces and the pursuit of spiritual enlightenment. In Satanic rituals, practitioners may trace the pentagram in the air or on the ground as a means of invoking protection, banishing negative energies, and aligning themselves with the natural rhythms of the universe.

In conclusion, symbolic acts and gestures play a crucial role in Satanic rituals, providing practitioners with powerful tools for communication, expression, and transformation. Through the use of symbolic imagery, gestures, and actions, practitioners are able to evoke specific states of consciousness, empower themselves, and facilitate personal growth and evolution. By exploring the meanings, purposes, and effects of symbolic acts and gestures in Satanic rituals, we gain insight into the rich tapestry of symbolism and meaning that underlies Satanic ritual practice, as well as its profound significance for practitioners.

## Rituals for Self-Reflection, Introspection, and Personal Growth

Rituals for self-reflection, introspection, and personal growth form an integral part of Satanic practice, providing practitioners with tools for deepening self-awareness, confronting inner truths, and fostering personal evolution. In this chapter, we explore the significance of rituals focused on self-reflection, introspection, and personal growth within the context of Satanism. These rituals serve as transformative experiences, enabling practitioners to gain insight into themselves, their beliefs, and their motivations.

Through an examination of rituals for self-reflection, introspection, and personal growth, we aim to unravel the methods and practices that enable Satanists to embark on the journey of self-discovery and self-mastery.

**The Importance of Self-Reflection in Satanic Rituals:**

Self-reflection is a cornerstone of Satanic philosophy, emphasizing the importance of introspection and self-examination in the pursuit of personal growth and empowerment. Satanic rituals often incorporate elements of self-reflection, inviting practitioners to examine their beliefs, values, and behaviors with honesty and clarity. These rituals provide opportunities for practitioners to confront their fears, doubts, and insecurities, and to embrace their strengths, passions, and aspirations.

Rituals for self-reflection may involve guided meditation, journaling exercises, or group discussions focused on exploring personal experiences, insights, and challenges. By engaging in practices of self-reflection, practitioners are able to gain insight into their own motivations, patterns of behavior, and underlying beliefs, enabling them to make informed choices and take deliberate action towards personal growth and fulfillment.

**The Practice of Introspection in Satanic Rituals:**

Introspection is another key practice in Satanic philosophy, encouraging practitioners to turn their gaze inward and explore the depths of their own psyche. Satanic rituals often provide opportunities for introspection, inviting practitioners to delve into their subconscious minds, confront inner demons, and unlock hidden potentials. These rituals may involve guided visualization exercises, inner journeying, or trance-inducing techniques designed to facilitate deep states of introspection and self-awareness.

Through the practice of introspection, practitioners are able to uncover hidden truths, release limiting beliefs, and tap into their inner resources. Introspective rituals provide opportunities for practitioners to connect with their authentic selves, cultivate self-acceptance and self-love, and align their actions with their deepest desires and values. By engaging in practices of introspection, Satanists are able to gain a deeper understanding of themselves and their place in the world, empowering them to live authentically and pursue their highest aspirations.

**Facilitating Personal Growth through Rituals:**

Rituals for personal growth are designed to help practitioners overcome obstacles, cultivate their talents, and become the best versions of themselves. These rituals provide opportunities for practitioners to set goals, clarify values, and develop strategies for personal development and achievement. Rituals for personal growth may involve visualization exercises, goal-setting rituals, or affirmations designed to reinforce positive beliefs and attitudes about oneself.

Through the practice of rituals for personal growth, practitioners are able to tap into their inner resources, overcome limiting beliefs, and embrace their inherent potential for greatness. Personal growth rituals provide opportunities for practitioners to expand their comfort zones, take calculated risks, and push themselves beyond perceived limitations. By engaging in practices of personal growth, Satanists are able to cultivate resilience, adaptability, and self-mastery, enabling them to thrive in the face of life's challenges and pursue their highest aspirations.

In conclusion, rituals for self-reflection, introspection, and personal growth are essential practices within the framework of Satanic philosophy, providing practitioners with tools for deepening self-awareness, confronting inner truths, and fostering personal evolution. Through the practice of these rituals, Satanists are able to gain insight into themselves, their beliefs, and their motivations, empowering them to make informed choices and take deliberate action towards personal growth and fulfillment. By embracing rituals for self-reflection, introspection, and personal growth, practitioners are able to embark on the journey of self-discovery and self-mastery, ultimately leading to a deeper sense of empowerment and purpose in life.

## Ceremonies for Commemoration

Ceremonies for commemoration hold a significant place within Satanic practice, providing practitioners with opportunities to honor significant events, milestones, or individuals in their lives from a Satanic perspective. In this chapter, we explore the importance of ceremonies for commemoration within the context of Satanism. These ceremonies serve as rituals of remembrance, celebration, and reflection, allowing practitioners to mark important moments in their personal journey and pay tribute to those who have influenced or inspired them. Through an examination of ceremonies for commemoration, we aim to unravel the significance of these rituals in Satanic philosophy and practice.

**Honoring Life Events:**

Ceremonies for commemoration in Satanism often revolve around honoring significant life events, such as births, weddings, or funerals, from a Satanic perspective. These ceremonies provide practitioners with opportunities to celebrate milestones, acknowledge achievements, and embrace transitions in their lives. Unlike traditional religious ceremonies, Satanic ceremonies for commemoration are often personalized and tailored to the individual's beliefs, values, and preferences.

For example, a Satanic ceremony for the birth of a child may involve rituals to invoke protection, blessings, and empowerment for the newborn and their parents. Similarly, a Satanic wedding ceremony may focus on themes of partnership, equality, and personal autonomy, emphasizing the importance of mutual respect and consent in the union.


**Remembering Influential Figures:**

Ceremonies for commemoration also serve as opportunities for practitioners to pay tribute to influential figures in Satanic history or their personal lives. These ceremonies may honor prominent Satanists, philosophers, artists, or activists who have made significant contributions to the advancement of Satanic philosophy and culture. By commemorating the lives and legacies of these individuals, practitioners seek to keep their memory alive and draw inspiration from their achievements and ideals.

For example, a ceremony for commemoration may be held to honor the life and teachings of Anton Szandor LaVey, the founder of The Church of Satan, or to pay tribute to other influential figures in Satanic history. These ceremonies may involve rituals of remembrance, readings of inspirational texts, or artistic performances dedicated to the memory of the individual being honored.

**Reflecting on Personal Growth:**

Ceremonies for commemoration also provide practitioners with opportunities to reflect on their personal growth and evolution over time. These ceremonies may mark anniversaries, milestones, or accomplishments in the individual's journey of self-discovery and self-mastery. By reflecting on their progress and achievements, practitioners gain a sense of perspective and gratitude for how far they have come on their path.

For example, a ceremony for commemoration may be held to celebrate the anniversary of a practitioner's initiation into Satanic philosophy or the completion of a significant personal goal. These ceremonies may involve rituals of reflection, journaling exercises, or guided meditations to honor the individual's growth and achievements and set intentions for the future.

In conclusion, ceremonies for commemoration play a vital role in Satanic practice, providing practitioners with opportunities to honor significant life events, remember influential figures, and reflect on personal growth and evolution. These ceremonies serve as rituals of remembrance, celebration, and reflection, allowing practitioners to mark important moments in their lives and pay tribute to those who have influenced or inspired them. By embracing ceremonies for commemoration, practitioners enrich their Satanic practice and deepen their connection to their beliefs, values, and community.

## Marking Life Events from a Satanic Perspective: Births, Weddings, Funerals, and Beyond

Marking life events from a Satanic perspective encompasses a unique approach to significant milestones such as births, weddings, funerals, and other important occasions. In this chapter, we delve into the significance of approaching these events within the framework of Satanic philosophy. Unlike traditional religious ceremonies, Satanic rituals for life events emphasize individualism, personal autonomy, and rationality. These ceremonies serve as opportunities for practitioners to celebrate, reflect, and honor life's transitions in alignment with Satanic principles. Through an exploration of marking life events from a Satanic perspective, we aim to unravel the significance of these rituals and their relevance to practitioners.

**Births:**

In Satanic philosophy, births are celebrated as moments of new beginnings, potential, and empowerment. Satanic ceremonies for births focus on welcoming the newborn into the world with love, protection, and empowerment. These ceremonies may involve rituals to invoke blessings, protection, and guidance for the child and their parents. Unlike traditional religious ceremonies, Satanic rituals for births are often personalized and tailored to the beliefs and values of the parents. For example, practitioners may perform rituals to affirm the child's individuality, strength, and autonomy, emphasizing their inherent worth and potential.

**Weddings:**

Satanic weddings are ceremonies of partnership, equality, and personal autonomy. Unlike traditional religious weddings, which may emphasize obedience, submission, and divine sanction, Satanic weddings celebrate the union of two individuals based on mutual respect, consent, and shared values. Satanic wedding ceremonies often involve rituals to affirm the couple's commitment to each other, celebrate their love and partnership, and empower them to build a life together based on their own terms. These ceremonies may include elements such as vows of mutual respect, exchange of symbolic tokens, and rituals to invoke blessings and protection for the couple's future.

**Funerals:**

Satanic funerals are ceremonies of remembrance, celebration, and reflection. Unlike traditional religious funerals, which may emphasize themes of sin, judgment, and divine redemption, Satanic funerals celebrate the life and legacy of the deceased with dignity and respect. Satanic funeral ceremonies focus on honoring the individual's contributions, achievements, and impact on the lives of others. These ceremonies may involve rituals of remembrance, readings of inspirational texts, and artistic performances dedicated to the memory of the deceased. Satanic funerals provide opportunities for practitioners to grieve, reflect, and find closure in their own way, without the need for religious dogma or supernatural beliefs.

**Beyond Births, Weddings, and Funerals:**

In addition to births, weddings, and funerals, Satanic philosophy offers a framework for marking other significant life events from a Satanic perspective. These may include coming-of-age ceremonies, career milestones, personal achievements, and other important occasions. Satanic rituals for these events emphasize individualism, personal empowerment, and rationality, providing practitioners with opportunities to celebrate, reflect, and honor their journey of self-discovery and self-mastery.

In conclusion, marking life events from a Satanic perspective offers practitioners a unique approach to celebrating, reflecting, and honoring significant milestones such as births, weddings, funerals, and beyond. Satanic rituals for life events emphasize individualism, personal autonomy, and rationality, providing practitioners with opportunities to align these moments with their beliefs, values, and principles. By embracing Satanic ceremonies for life events, practitioners enrich their connection to their beliefs, values, and community, ultimately leading to a deeper sense of empowerment and fulfillment in life.

## Rituals to Honor Milestones and Celebrate Personal Achievements

Rituals to honor milestones and celebrate personal achievements are integral to Satanic practice, providing practitioners with opportunities to acknowledge their growth, success, and progress on their journey of self-discovery and self-mastery. In this chapter, we explore the significance of these rituals within the context of Satanic philosophy. These rituals serve as moments of reflection, empowerment, and self-affirmation, allowing practitioners to recognize their accomplishments and reaffirm their commitment to their goals and values. Through an examination of rituals to honor milestones and celebrate personal achievements, we aim to unravel the methods and practices that enable Satanists to acknowledge and celebrate their successes.

**Acknowledging Personal Growth:**

Rituals to honor milestones and celebrate personal achievements are designed to acknowledge and celebrate the progress and growth of practitioners on their individual paths. These rituals provide opportunities for practitioners to reflect on their journey, recognize their accomplishments, and express gratitude for their efforts and achievements. Whether it's completing a significant project, reaching a career milestone, or overcoming a personal challenge, these rituals offer moments of validation and affirmation for practitioners.

For example, a ritual to honor a career milestone may involve reflecting on the skills, knowledge, and experience gained throughout one's career journey, acknowledging the challenges overcome and the achievements attained. Similarly, a ritual to celebrate personal growth may involve reflecting on the lessons learned, the obstacles overcome, and the personal transformations experienced on the path of self-discovery and self-mastery.

**Affirming Personal Values:**

Rituals to honor milestones and celebrate personal achievements also serve as opportunities for practitioners to reaffirm their commitment to their values, goals, and aspirations. These rituals provide moments of alignment and reconnection with one's core beliefs and principles, strengthening the practitioner's resolve and determination to continue on their chosen path. By celebrating their achievements in a ritualized context, practitioners reinforce the importance of their values and the significance of their goals in their lives.

For example, a ritual to celebrate a personal achievement may involve reaffirming one's dedication to Satanic principles such as individualism, rationalism, and personal autonomy. Through rituals of affirmation and recommitment, practitioners deepen their connection to their values and draw strength and inspiration from their achievements.

**Fostering Community and Support:**

Rituals to honor milestones and celebrate personal achievements also play a crucial role in fostering community and support among practitioners. These rituals provide opportunities for practitioners to share their successes, experiences, and aspirations with others, building connections and camaraderie within the Satanic community. By celebrating their achievements together, practitioners create a supportive environment where they can encourage and uplift each other on their individual paths.

For example, a ritual to honor a milestone may involve sharing stories of personal triumphs and challenges, offering words of encouragement and support to fellow practitioners, and collectively celebrating the achievements of the community as a whole. Through rituals of community and support, practitioners strengthen their bonds with each other and create a sense of belonging and solidarity within the Satanic community.

In conclusion, rituals to honor milestones and celebrate personal achievements are essential practices within the framework of Satanic philosophy, providing practitioners with opportunities to acknowledge their growth, success, and progress on their journey of self-discovery and self-mastery. These rituals serve as moments of reflection, empowerment, and affirmation, allowing practitioners to recognize their accomplishments, reaffirm their commitment to their values, and foster community and support within the Satanic community. By embracing these rituals, practitioners enrich their connection to their beliefs, values, and community, ultimately leading to a deeper sense of empowerment and fulfillment in life.

# Group Gatherings and Community Building

Group gatherings and community building are vital components of Satanic practice, providing practitioners with opportunities to connect, share experiences, and support each other on their individual paths. In this chapter, we delve into the significance of group gatherings and community building within the context of Satanic philosophy. These gatherings serve as platforms for collaboration, camaraderie, and mutual empowerment, fostering a sense of belonging and solidarity among practitioners. Through an exploration of group gatherings and community building, we aim to unravel the methods and practices that enable Satanists to come together, forge connections, and build strong, supportive communities.

**The Importance of Group Gatherings:**

Group gatherings play a crucial role in Satanic practice, providing practitioners with opportunities to come together in person or virtually to discuss philosophy, share experiences, and engage in rituals and activities. These gatherings serve as forums for intellectual exchange, creative expression, and personal growth, allowing practitioners to learn from each other, challenge their assumptions, and broaden their perspectives. By participating in group gatherings, practitioners deepen their understanding of Satanic philosophy and strengthen their connections to the Satanic community.

Group gatherings may take various forms, including meetings, study groups, workshops, rituals, social events, and activism initiatives. These gatherings provide opportunities for practitioners to explore different aspects of Satanic philosophy, engage in collaborative projects, and build lasting friendships and alliances with like-minded individuals. Whether it's discussing philosophical concepts, practicing rituals together, or working towards common goals, group gatherings foster a sense of camaraderie and mutual support among practitioners.

**Fostering Community Building:**

Community building is a central focus of Satanic philosophy, emphasizing the importance of creating strong, supportive communities where individuals can thrive and grow. Satanic practitioners place a high value on individualism and personal autonomy, but they also recognize the power of coming together as a community to achieve common goals and support each other in times of need. Community building involves creating inclusive spaces where practitioners feel welcome, respected, and valued for who they are.

Community building efforts may include organizing regular group gatherings, creating online forums and social media groups, and participating in community outreach and activism initiatives. These efforts help to create opportunities for practitioners to connect, share resources, and support each other on their individual paths. By fostering a sense of belonging and solidarity within the Satanic community, community building initiatives empower practitioners to live authentically and pursue their highest aspirations.

**Promoting Diversity and Inclusivity:**

Diversity and inclusivity are fundamental values of Satanic philosophy, emphasizing the importance of embracing and celebrating differences among individuals. Satanic communities strive to create spaces where practitioners from diverse backgrounds, identities, and experiences feel welcome and valued. Community building efforts focus on promoting diversity and inclusivity within the Satanic community, ensuring that all practitioners have a voice and a place at the table.

Community building initiatives may include organizing events and activities that celebrate diverse perspectives and experiences, creating resources and support networks for marginalized individuals, and advocating for social justice and equality within and beyond the Satanic community. By promoting diversity and inclusivity, Satanic communities enrich their collective experience, foster empathy and understanding, and create a more vibrant and resilient community for all practitioners.

In conclusion, group gatherings and community building are essential practices within the framework of Satanic philosophy, providing practitioners with opportunities to connect, share experiences, and support each other on their individual paths.

These gatherings foster a sense of belonging and solidarity among practitioners, empowering them to live authentically and pursue their highest aspirations. By embracing diversity and inclusivity and fostering strong, supportive communities, Satanic practitioners enrich their connection to their beliefs, values, and community, ultimately leading to a deeper sense of empowerment and fulfillment in life.

## The Importance of Community in Satanic Practice

Community plays a pivotal role in Satanic practice, serving as a source of support, camaraderie, and empowerment for practitioners. In this chapter, we explore the significance of community within the framework of Satanic philosophy. Satanic communities provide practitioners with opportunities to connect, share experiences, and collaborate on shared goals and values. Through an examination of the importance of community in Satanic practice, we aim to unravel the ways in which community enriches the Satanic experience and empowers practitioners on their individual paths.

**Building Support Networks:**

One of the key functions of community in Satanic practice is the establishment of support networks among practitioners. Satanic communities provide spaces where individuals can find understanding, validation, and encouragement from like-minded peers. These support networks offer emotional support during times of difficulty, practical assistance in achieving goals, and opportunities for personal growth and development.

Support networks within Satanic communities may take various forms, including online forums, social media groups, local meetups, and organized events. These platforms enable practitioners to connect with others who share their beliefs and values, fostering a sense of camaraderie and solidarity among community members. By building support networks, Satanic communities empower practitioners to navigate life's challenges with greater resilience, confidence, and determination.

**Fostering Intellectual Exchange:**

Satanic communities serve as hubs for intellectual exchange, debate, and exploration of ideas. Within these communities, practitioners engage in discussions on a wide range of topics, including philosophy, ethics, politics, and culture. These conversations provide opportunities for practitioners to challenge their assumptions, expand their perspectives, and deepen their understanding of Satanic philosophy and its implications for their lives.

Intellectual exchange within Satanic communities may occur through various channels, including online forums, study groups, book clubs, and organized events such as lectures or debates. These platforms facilitate the exchange of ideas and insights among practitioners, fostering a culture of critical thinking, curiosity, and open-mindedness. By fostering intellectual exchange, Satanic communities empower practitioners to refine their beliefs, articulate their values, and develop a more nuanced understanding of the world around them.

**Creating Spaces for Expression and Creativity:**

Satanic communities provide spaces for practitioners to express themselves creatively and explore their passions and interests. These communities embrace diversity and individualism, celebrating the unique talents, perspectives, and contributions of each member. Whether through art, music, writing, or other forms of creative expression, practitioners have the opportunity to share their creativity with others and contribute to the vibrant cultural landscape of the Satanic community.

Creative expression within Satanic communities may take various forms, including art exhibitions, music performances, literary publications, and collaborative projects. These platforms provide practitioners with opportunities to showcase their work, connect with fellow artists and creators, and inspire others with their vision and creativity. By creating spaces for expression and creativity, Satanic communities empower practitioners to embrace their uniqueness, unleash their creative potential, and make meaningful contributions to the community and the world at large.

In conclusion, the importance of community in Satanic practice cannot be overstated. Satanic communities serve as sources of support, camaraderie, and empowerment for practitioners, providing spaces where individuals can connect, share experiences, and collaborate on shared goals and values. Through building support networks, fostering intellectual exchange, and creating spaces for expression and creativity, Satanic communities enrich the Satanic experience and empower practitioners on their individual paths. By embracing community, practitioners strengthen their connection to their beliefs, values, and community, ultimately leading to a deeper sense of empowerment and fulfillment in life.

# Rituals for Group Bonding, Discussion, and Support

Rituals for group bonding, discussion, and support are essential components of Satanic practice, providing practitioners with opportunities to connect, share experiences, and offer support to one another. In this chapter, we delve into the significance of these rituals within the framework of Satanic philosophy. These rituals serve as catalysts for building strong, supportive communities where practitioners can find camaraderie, engage in intellectual exchange, and receive encouragement and validation from their peers. Through an exploration of rituals for group bonding, discussion, and support, we aim to unravel the methods and practices that enable Satanists to foster meaningful connections and create a sense of belonging within their communities.

**Fostering Group Bonding:**

Rituals for group bonding are designed to strengthen the connections and camaraderie among practitioners within the Satanic community. These rituals provide opportunities for practitioners to come together in person or virtually to engage in shared experiences, forge friendships, and build a sense of belonging. Group bonding rituals may include activities such as group meals, game nights, outdoor adventures, or other social gatherings that allow practitioners to relax, have fun, and get to know each other on a deeper level.

Group bonding rituals create spaces where practitioners can let down their guard, share laughs, and form lasting bonds with like-minded individuals. These rituals foster a sense of community and solidarity, empowering practitioners to support each other, collaborate on shared goals, and celebrate their successes together. By fostering group bonding, Satanic communities create environments where practitioners feel valued, respected, and accepted for who they are.

**Facilitating Intellectual Exchange:**

Rituals for group discussion are platforms for intellectual exchange, debate, and exploration of ideas within the Satanic community. These rituals provide opportunities for practitioners to engage in thought-provoking conversations on a wide range of topics, including philosophy, ethics, politics, and culture. Group discussion rituals may take various forms, including study groups, book clubs, or organized events such as lectures or debates, where practitioners can share insights, challenge assumptions, and expand their perspectives.

Group discussion rituals create spaces where practitioners can engage in critical thinking, articulate their beliefs, and refine their understanding of Satanic philosophy and its implications for their lives. These rituals foster a culture of curiosity, open-mindedness, and respectful dialogue, empowering practitioners to explore complex ideas and concepts in a supportive environment. By facilitating intellectual exchange, Satanic communities empower practitioners to develop their intellectual faculties, deepen their understanding of the world around them, and articulate their values with clarity and conviction.

**Providing Emotional Support:**

Rituals for group support are designed to provide emotional support, validation, and encouragement to practitioners within the Satanic community. These rituals create spaces where practitioners can share their experiences, express their feelings, and receive empathy and understanding from their peers. Group support rituals may include activities such as support circles, peer counseling sessions, or other structured formats where practitioners can offer and receive support in a safe and non-judgmental environment.

Group support rituals help practitioners navigate life's challenges, cope with stress, and overcome obstacles on their individual paths. These rituals foster a culture of empathy, compassion, and mutual aid, empowering practitioners to lean on each other for strength and resilience in times of need. By providing emotional support, Satanic communities create spaces where practitioners feel heard, valued, and supported as they navigate the complexities of existence.

In conclusion, rituals for group bonding, discussion, and support are essential practices within the framework of Satanic philosophy, providing practitioners with opportunities to connect, engage in intellectual exchange, and offer support to one another. These rituals foster meaningful connections, create a sense of belonging, and empower practitioners to navigate life's challenges with resilience and strength. By embracing rituals for group bonding, discussion, and support, Satanic communities create environments where practitioners feel valued, respected, and supported on their individual paths.

## Satanic Holidays and Observances

Satanic holidays and observances hold a significant place within Satanic practice, providing practitioners with opportunities to commemorate important dates, honor Satanic figures, and celebrate key aspects of Satanic philosophy and culture. In this chapter, we delve into the significance of Satanic holidays and observances within the framework of Satanic philosophy. These holidays serve as occasions for reflection, celebration, and ritualized practice, allowing practitioners to deepen their connection to their beliefs, values, and community. Through an exploration of Satanic holidays and observances, we aim to unravel the traditions, symbolism, and rituals associated with these significant dates in the Satanic calendar.

**The Philosophy of Satanic Holidays:**

Satanic holidays are rooted in the principles of individualism, personal empowerment, and rationalism, reflecting key aspects of Satanic philosophy and culture. Unlike traditional religious holidays, which may emphasize obedience, submission, and divine worship, Satanic holidays celebrate themes such as rebellion, independence, and self-expression. These holidays serve as reminders of the importance of asserting one's autonomy, embracing one's uniqueness, and living life on one's own terms.

Satanic holidays are often associated with significant events in Satanic history or mythology, such as the founding of The Church of Satan or the publication of key Satanic texts. These holidays provide opportunities for practitioners to reflect on the achievements and contributions of Satanic figures, honor their legacies, and draw inspiration from their teachings. By commemorating Satanic holidays, practitioners reaffirm their commitment to Satanic principles and strengthen their connection to the Satanic community.

**Key Satanic Holidays and Observances:**

There are several key Satanic holidays and observances that hold special significance within the Satanic calendar. These holidays may vary among different Satanic traditions and organizations, but they often share common themes and symbolism associated with Satanic philosophy and culture. Some of the most notable Satanic holidays and observances include:

**Walpurgisnacht:** Celebrated on April 30th, Walpurgisnacht is a night of revelry and celebration in Satanic tradition. It is often associated with themes of fertility, vitality, and the triumph of life over death. Practitioners may engage in rituals to invoke energy, vitality, and creativity, or celebrate with gatherings, feasts, and performances.

**Halloween:** Halloween, or Samhain, is a widely celebrated holiday in Satanic tradition, marking the end of the harvest season and the beginning of the dark half of the year. It is a time for honoring the dead, reflecting on mortality, and embracing the mysteries of the unknown. Practitioners may engage in rituals to honor ancestors, commune with spirits, or explore themes of death and rebirth.

**Satanic New Year:** The Satanic New Year, often celebrated on the anniversary of the founding of The Church of Satan on April 30th, is a time for reflection, renewal, and goal-setting. It marks the beginning of a new cycle of growth and evolution for practitioners, who may engage in rituals to set intentions, release the past, and embrace new beginnings.

**Unholy Days:** Unholy Days are specific dates throughout the year that hold significance within Satanic tradition, such as the birthdays of prominent Satanic figures or other events of historical or cultural importance. Practitioners may choose to commemorate these days with rituals, celebrations, or acts of personal significance that align with Satanic values and principles.

**Rituals and Traditions:**

Satanic holidays and observances are often marked by rituals, traditions, and symbolic acts that reflect the themes and symbolism associated with Satanic philosophy and culture. These rituals may include invocations, meditations, symbolic gestures, or ceremonial practices designed to evoke energy, focus intention, and deepen connection to Satanic principles.

For example, rituals for Walpurgisnacht may involve bonfires, music, dancing, and other forms of revelry to celebrate vitality and life force. Rituals for Halloween may include offerings to ancestors, divination practices, or symbolic acts of death and rebirth to honor the cycle of life and death. Satanic New Year rituals may involve reflection on personal growth and accomplishments, setting intentions for the future, and renewing commitment to Satanic values.

In conclusion, Satanic holidays and observances play a vital role in Satanic practice, providing practitioners with opportunities to commemorate important dates, honor Satanic figures, and celebrate key aspects of Satanic philosophy and culture. These holidays serve as occasions for reflection, celebration, and ritualized practice, allowing practitioners to deepen their connection to their beliefs, values, and community. By embracing Satanic holidays and observances, practitioners enrich their Satanic experience and strengthen their connection to the Satanic tradition.

## Exploring Significant Dates and Events in Satanic History

Significant dates and events in Satanic history hold a special place within Satanic practice, serving as markers of important milestones, achievements, and cultural developments within the Satanic tradition. In this chapter, we delve into the significance of these dates and events within the framework of Satanic philosophy. From the founding of The Church of Satan to the publication of key Satanic texts, these events have shaped the course of Satanic history and continue to influence the beliefs, practices, and culture of modern Satanic communities. Through an exploration of significant dates and events in Satanic history, we aim to unravel the rich tapestry of Satanic tradition and its evolution over time.

**The Founding of The Church of Satan:**

One of the most significant events in Satanic history is the founding of The Church of Satan by Anton Szandor LaVey on April 30, 1966. This event marked the beginning of organized Satanic practice and the formalization of Satanic philosophy into a coherent belief system. LaVey's creation of The Church of Satan provided a platform for practitioners to come together, share ideas, and explore Satanic principles in a structured and organized manner. The founding of The Church of Satan remains a foundational moment in Satanic history, symbolizing the emergence of a new religious movement dedicated to the celebration of individualism, personal empowerment, and rationalism.

**The Publication of "The Satanic Bible":**

Another significant event in Satanic history is the publication of "The Satanic Bible" by Anton Szandor LaVey in 1969. "The Satanic Bible" serves as the central text of Satanic philosophy, outlining key principles, rituals, and practices for practitioners to follow. LaVey's publication of "The Satanic Bible" brought Satanic philosophy to a wider audience and provided practitioners with a comprehensive guide to Satanic practice. The book continues to be a cornerstone of Satanic literature and a source of inspiration for generations of practitioners around the world.

**The Evolution of Satanic Thought and Practice:**

Throughout its history, Satanic thought and practice have continued to evolve and adapt to changing cultural, social, and political contexts. Satanic communities have emerged in various forms, each with its own interpretations of Satanic philosophy and unique approaches to ritual and practice. From the emergence of LaVeyan Satanism to the rise of contemporary Satanic organizations such as The Satanic Temple, Satanic thought and practice have diversified and expanded to encompass a wide range of beliefs, values, and practices.

**Key Figures in Satanic History:**

Several key figures have played instrumental roles in shaping the course of Satanic history and advancing the principles of Satanic philosophy. Anton Szandor LaVey, the founder of The Church of Satan, remains one of the most influential figures in Satanic history, known for his charismatic leadership and groundbreaking contributions to Satanic thought and practice. Other notable figures include Michael A. Aquino, founder of the Temple of Set, and Lucien Greaves, co-founder of The Satanic Temple, who have each made significant contributions to the development of modern Satanic thought and practice.

In conclusion, significant dates and events in Satanic history hold a special place within Satanic practice, serving as markers of important milestones, achievements, and cultural developments within the Satanic tradition. From the founding of The Church of

Satan to the publication of key Satanic texts, these events have shaped the course of Satanic history and continue to influence the beliefs, practices, and culture of modern Satanic communities. By exploring significant dates and events in Satanic history, practitioners gain a deeper understanding of the rich tapestry of Satanic tradition and its evolution over time.

## Rituals and Traditions for Observing Satanic Holidays and Festivals

Rituals and traditions for observing Satanic holidays and festivals are integral components of Satanic practice, providing practitioners with opportunities to commemorate important dates, honor Satanic figures, and celebrate key aspects of Satanic philosophy and culture. In this chapter, we delve into the significance of these rituals and traditions within the framework of Satanic philosophy. From Walpurgisnacht to Halloween, these holidays and festivals serve as occasions for reflection, celebration, and ritualized practice, allowing practitioners to deepen their connection to their beliefs, values, and community. Through an exploration of rituals and traditions for observing Satanic holidays and festivals, we aim to unravel the methods and practices that enable practitioners to enrich their Satanic experience and strengthen their connection to the Satanic tradition.

**Understanding Satanic Holidays and Festivals:**

Satanic holidays and festivals are rooted in the principles of individualism, personal empowerment, and rationalism, reflecting key aspects of Satanic philosophy and culture. Unlike traditional religious holidays, which may emphasize obedience, submission, and divine worship, Satanic holidays celebrate themes such as rebellion, independence, and self-expression. These holidays serve as reminders of the importance of asserting one's autonomy, embracing one's uniqueness, and living life on one's own terms.

Satanic holidays and festivals may vary among different Satanic traditions and organizations, but they often share common themes and symbolism associated with Satanic philosophy and culture. Some of the most notable Satanic holidays and festivals include Walpurgisnacht, Halloween, and the Satanic New Year. These holidays provide opportunities for practitioners to reflect on the achievements and contributions of Satanic figures, honor their legacies, and draw inspiration from their teachings.

**Rituals and Traditions:**

Rituals and traditions for observing Satanic holidays and festivals may include a variety of practices, ceremonies, and symbolic acts designed to evoke energy, focus intention, and deepen connection to Satanic principles. These rituals may vary depending on the specific holiday or festival being observed, but they often share common elements and themes associated with Satanic philosophy and culture.

For example, rituals for Walpurgisnacht may involve bonfires, music, dancing, and other forms of revelry to celebrate vitality and life force. Rituals for Halloween may include offerings to ancestors, divination practices, or symbolic acts of death and rebirth to honor the cycle of life and death. Satanic New Year rituals may involve reflection on personal growth and accomplishments, setting intentions for the future, and renewing commitment to Satanic values.

In addition to rituals, traditions for observing Satanic holidays and festivals may include practices such as decorating altars or shrines with symbolic imagery, preparing and sharing special meals or offerings, and engaging in acts of creativity or self-expression that align with Satanic principles and values. These traditions help to create a sense of continuity and connection to Satanic tradition, allowing practitioners to honor the past, celebrate the present, and envision the future of Satanic practice.

In conclusion, rituals and traditions for observing Satanic holidays and festivals are integral components of Satanic practice, providing practitioners with opportunities to commemorate important dates, honor Satanic figures, and celebrate key aspects of Satanic philosophy and culture. These rituals and traditions serve as occasions for reflection, celebration, and ritualized practice, allowing practitioners to deepen their connection to their beliefs, values, and community. By embracing rituals and traditions for observing Satanic holidays and festivals, practitioners enrich their Satanic experience and strengthen their connection to the Satanic tradition.

## Destruction and Symbolic Rebirth

Destruction and symbolic rebirth are powerful themes within Satanic philosophy, representing processes of transformation, renewal, and personal growth. In this chapter, we explore the significance of destruction and symbolic rebirth within the framework of Satanic practice. These concepts emphasize the importance of releasing the old, embracing change, and embracing the potential for growth and evolution. Through an exploration of destruction and symbolic rebirth, we aim to unravel the methods and practices that enable practitioners to navigate life's challenges, overcome obstacles, and emerge stronger and more resilient on their individual paths.

**The Concept of Destruction:**

In Satanic philosophy, destruction is not necessarily about causing harm or chaos but rather about breaking down barriers, limitations, and obstacles that hinder personal growth and development. Destruction represents the process of letting go of old beliefs, patterns, and behaviors that no longer serve one's highest good. It is about shedding the layers of conditioning and conformity imposed by society and embracing one's true nature and potential.

Destruction rituals in Satanic practice may involve symbolic acts of breaking, tearing, or burning to represent the dismantling of barriers and limitations. These rituals are often accompanied by affirmations or intentions to release negative energy, clear away obstacles, and create space for new possibilities to emerge. By embracing destruction, practitioners empower themselves to confront their fears, confront their limitations, and embrace change as a catalyst for personal growth and transformation.

**The Symbolism of Rebirth:**

Symbolic rebirth is a central theme within Satanic philosophy, representing the process of transformation, renewal, and personal evolution. Rebirth is about embracing the potential for growth and change, and emerging from challenges and setbacks stronger, wiser, and more resilient than before. It is about tapping into one's inner power and potential and harnessing it to create a new reality that aligns with one's true desires and aspirations.

Rebirth rituals in Satanic practice may involve symbolic acts of renewal, such as purification rituals, rebirthing ceremonies, or rites of passage that mark significant transitions in one's life. These rituals are often accompanied by affirmations or intentions to embrace change, cultivate resilience, and manifest one's highest potential. By embracing symbolic rebirth, practitioners empower themselves to embrace their true selves, overcome adversity, and create a life that is in alignment with their deepest values and aspirations.

**Integration and Synthesis:**

The concepts of destruction and symbolic rebirth are not about erasing the past or denying one's history, but rather about integrating and synthesizing one's experiences into a coherent and empowering narrative. Destruction and rebirth are part of a continuous cycle of growth and evolution, where each experience builds upon the last, and each challenge becomes an opportunity for learning and growth.

In Satanic practice, practitioners are encouraged to embrace both the light and the dark aspects of their nature, and to recognize that transformation and growth often emerge from the depths of adversity. By embracing destruction and symbolic rebirth, practitioners empower themselves to confront their fears, confront their limitations, and embrace change as a catalyst for personal growth and transformation.

In conclusion, destruction and symbolic rebirth are powerful themes within Satanic philosophy, representing processes of transformation, renewal, and personal growth. These concepts emphasize the importance of releasing the old, embracing change, and harnessing the potential for growth and evolution. By embracing destruction and symbolic rebirth, practitioners empower themselves to confront their fears, confront their limitations, and emerge stronger and more resilient on their individual paths. Through an exploration of destruction and symbolic rebirth, practitioners deepen their connection to Satanic philosophy and cultivate the inner strength and resilience needed to navigate life's challenges and embrace their true potential.

# Understanding Destruction Rituals in Satanic Practice

Destruction rituals hold a significant place within Satanic practice, serving as powerful tools for personal transformation, empowerment, and growth. In this chapter, we delve into the significance of destruction rituals within the framework of Satanic philosophy. These rituals are not about causing harm or chaos but rather about breaking down barriers, limitations, and obstacles that hinder personal development. Through an exploration of destruction rituals, we aim to unravel the methods and practices that enable practitioners to confront their fears, release negative energy, and embrace change as a catalyst for personal growth and transformation.

**The Purpose of Destruction Rituals:**

In Satanic philosophy, destruction rituals are symbolic acts of releasing the old, letting go of outdated beliefs, patterns, and behaviors, and creating space for new possibilities to emerge. These rituals are about breaking free from societal conditioning, conformity, and expectations, and embracing one's true nature and potential. Destruction rituals empower practitioners to confront their fears, confront their limitations, and embrace change as a pathway to personal growth and empowerment.

The purpose of destruction rituals is not to cause harm or chaos but rather to create a sense of catharsis, liberation, and renewal. These rituals provide practitioners with opportunities to release pent-up emotions, clear away negative energy, and cultivate a sense of inner peace and clarity. By embracing destruction rituals, practitioners empower themselves to confront their fears, confront their limitations, and emerge stronger and more resilient on their individual paths.

**Methods and Practices:**

Destruction rituals in Satanic practice may take various forms, from simple acts of destruction such as breaking, tearing, or burning, to more elaborate ceremonies and rites. The key is to choose methods and practices that resonate with the practitioner's intentions and goals and align with the principles of Satanic philosophy.

**Some common methods and practices of destruction rituals include:**

Symbolic acts of destruction, such as breaking objects, tearing up papers, or burning symbolic representations of barriers, limitations, or negative energy.

Visualization techniques, where practitioners imagine themselves breaking free from obstacles and limitations, releasing negative energy, and embracing change and transformation.

Affirmations and intentions, where practitioners vocalize their intentions to release the old, let go of outdated beliefs and behaviors, and embrace new possibilities and opportunities for growth.

Ritualized ceremonies and rites, where practitioners engage in structured rituals and ceremonies to mark significant transitions, such as the end of a chapter in life, the release of past traumas, or the initiation of a new phase of personal development.

In conclusion, destruction rituals are powerful tools for personal transformation, empowerment, and growth within Satanic practice. These rituals provide practitioners with opportunities to confront their fears, release negative energy, and embrace change as a catalyst for personal growth and transformation. By embracing destruction rituals, practitioners empower themselves to break free from barriers, limitations, and obstacles that hinder their development and emerge stronger and more resilient on their individual paths. Through an exploration of destruction rituals, practitioners deepen their connection to Satanic philosophy and cultivate the inner strength and resilience needed to navigate life's challenges and embrace their true potential.

## Rituals for Symbolic Rebirth, Transformation, and Renewal

Rituals for symbolic rebirth, transformation, and renewal are integral components of Satanic practice, providing practitioners with opportunities to embrace change, release the old, and cultivate a sense of empowerment and renewal. In this chapter, we delve into the significance of these rituals within the framework of Satanic philosophy. These rituals symbolize the process of shedding old beliefs, patterns, and behaviors that no longer serve one's highest good, and embracing new possibilities for growth, evolution, and personal empowerment. Through an exploration of rituals for symbolic rebirth, transformation, and renewal, we aim to unravel the methods and practices that enable practitioners to navigate life's challenges, overcome obstacles, and emerge stronger and more resilient on their individual paths.

**Understanding Symbolic Rebirth:**

Symbolic rebirth is a central theme within Satanic philosophy, representing the process of transformation, renewal, and personal evolution. It is about letting go of the past, releasing outdated beliefs and patterns, and embracing new opportunities for growth, change, and empowerment. Symbolic rebirth rituals provide practitioners with opportunities to shed the layers of conditioning and conformity imposed by society and reconnect with their true selves and potential.

Symbolic rebirth rituals may involve acts of purification, renewal, and transformation, such as bathing in sacred waters, anointing oneself with oils or herbs, or engaging in visualization exercises to imagine oneself emerging from a cocoon or chrysalis, transformed and renewed. These rituals are often accompanied by affirmations or intentions to release the old, let go of outdated beliefs and behaviors, and embrace new possibilities for growth and empowerment.

**Methods and Practices:**

Rituals for symbolic rebirth, transformation, and renewal may take various forms, from simple acts of purification and cleansing to more elaborate ceremonies and rites. The key is to choose methods and practices that resonate with the practitioner's intentions and goals and align with the principles of Satanic philosophy.

**Some common methods and practices of rituals for symbolic rebirth, transformation, and renewal include:**

Purification rituals, where practitioners engage in acts of cleansing and purification to release negative energy, clear away obstacles, and create space for new possibilities to emerge. This may include bathing in sacred waters, smudging with herbs or incense, or anointing oneself with oils or essences.

Visualization techniques, where practitioners imagine themselves shedding old beliefs and patterns, and emerging transformed and renewed. This may involve guided meditations, visualizations of rebirth symbols such as the phoenix or the serpent shedding its skin, or creative visualization exercises to manifest desired outcomes and possibilities.

Affirmations and intentions, where practitioners vocalize their intentions to release the old, let go of outdated beliefs and behaviors, and embrace new opportunities for growth and empowerment. This may involve repeating affirmations or mantras that affirm one's worthiness, resilience, and potential, and reinforce the belief in one's ability to transform and renew.

Ritualized ceremonies and rites, where practitioners engage in structured rituals and ceremonies to mark significant transitions, such as the end of a chapter in life, the release of past traumas, or the initiation of a new phase of personal development. This may include rites of passage, initiation ceremonies, or symbolic acts of transformation such as burying old objects or writing down limiting beliefs and burning them in a ritual fire.

In conclusion, rituals for symbolic rebirth, transformation, and renewal are integral components of Satanic practice, providing practitioners with opportunities to embrace change, release the old, and cultivate a sense of empowerment and renewal. These rituals symbolize the process of shedding old beliefs, patterns, and behaviors that no longer serve one's highest good, and embracing new possibilities for growth, evolution, and personal empowerment. By embracing rituals for symbolic rebirth, transformation, and renewal, practitioners empower themselves to navigate life's challenges, overcome obstacles, and emerge stronger and more resilient on their individual paths. Through an exploration of these rituals, practitioners deepen their connection to Satanic philosophy and cultivate the inner strength and resilience needed to embrace their true potential.

# Protection and Empowerment

Protection and empowerment are fundamental principles within Satanic philosophy, emphasizing the importance of personal sovereignty, self-defense, and empowerment. In this chapter, we explore the significance of protection and empowerment within the framework of Satanic practice. These concepts emphasize the importance of asserting one's autonomy, defending against external threats, and cultivating inner strength and resilience. Through an exploration of protection and empowerment, we aim to unravel the methods and practices that enable practitioners to safeguard their well-being, assert their boundaries, and thrive in the face of adversity.

**Understanding Protection:**

Protection in Satanic philosophy is not about passive defense or avoidance but rather about actively asserting one's boundaries, defending against external threats, and cultivating a sense of inner strength and resilience. It is about recognizing one's inherent worth and value and taking proactive steps to safeguard one's well-being and autonomy. Protection rituals and practices in Satanic practice are designed to create a shield of energy and intention around oneself, deflecting negativity and harm and empowering practitioners to navigate life's challenges with confidence and resilience.

Protection rituals may involve acts of visualization, where practitioners imagine themselves surrounded by a shield of protective energy, or the invocation of protective symbols or entities to ward off negative influences. These rituals are often accompanied by affirmations or intentions to assert one's boundaries, defend against external threats, and cultivate a sense of inner strength and resilience. By embracing protection rituals, practitioners empower themselves to assert their autonomy, defend against external threats, and create a safe and supportive environment in which to thrive.

**Understanding Empowerment:**

Empowerment in Satanic philosophy is about recognizing and embracing one's innate power and potential and using it to create a life that aligns with one's deepest desires and aspirations. It is about taking ownership of one's life and choices, and refusing to be defined or limited by external expectations or constraints. Empowerment rituals and practices in Satanic practice are designed to cultivate a sense of self-confidence, agency, and resilience, empowering practitioners to pursue their goals and dreams with courage and conviction.

Empowerment rituals may involve acts of self-affirmation, where practitioners vocalize their strengths, talents, and abilities, or the visualization of oneself as a powerful and unstoppable force for positive change. These rituals are often accompanied by affirmations or intentions to embrace one's power, overcome obstacles, and manifest one's desires and aspirations. By embracing empowerment rituals, practitioners empower themselves to take control of their lives, pursue their goals with confidence and determination, and create a reality that reflects their deepest values and aspirations.

**Methods and Practices:**

Protection and empowerment rituals in Satanic practice may take various forms, from simple acts of visualization and affirmation to more elaborate ceremonies and rites. The key is to choose methods and practices that resonate with the practitioner's intentions and goals and align with the principles of Satanic philosophy.

**Some common methods and practices of protection and empowerment rituals include:**

Visualization techniques, where practitioners imagine themselves surrounded by a shield of protective energy or visualize themselves as powerful and unstoppable beings capable of overcoming any obstacle.

Affirmations and intentions, where practitioners vocalize their intentions to assert their boundaries, defend against external threats, and cultivate a sense of inner strength and resilience.

Ritualized ceremonies and rites, where practitioners engage in structured rituals and ceremonies to mark significant transitions, such as the initiation of a new phase of personal development or the pursuit of a specific goal or aspiration.

In conclusion, protection and empowerment are fundamental principles within Satanic philosophy, emphasizing the importance of personal sovereignty, self-defense, and empowerment. Through rituals and practices of protection and empowerment, practitioners empower themselves to assert their autonomy, defend against external threats, and create a life that aligns with their deepest desires and aspirations. By embracing protection and empowerment, practitioners cultivate a sense of inner strength and resilience, enabling them to navigate life's challenges with confidence and determination. Through an exploration of protection and empowerment, practitioners deepen their connection to Satanic philosophy and cultivate the inner strength and resilience needed to thrive in an often challenging world.

## Rituals for Personal Protection, Empowerment, and Defense

Rituals for personal protection, empowerment, and defense are essential practices within Satanic philosophy, aimed at safeguarding practitioners' well-being, asserting their autonomy, and cultivating inner strength and resilience. In this chapter, we explore the significance of these rituals within the framework of Satanic practice. These rituals serve to create a shield of energy and intention around practitioners, deflecting negativity, asserting boundaries, and empowering them to navigate life's challenges with confidence and resilience. Through an exploration of rituals for personal protection, empowerment, and defense, we aim to unravel the methods and practices that enable practitioners to thrive in the face of adversity and adversity.

**Understanding Personal Protection:**

Personal protection in Satanic philosophy involves actively safeguarding one's well-being, asserting boundaries, and defending against external threats or negative influences. It is about recognizing one's inherent worth and value and taking proactive steps to ensure one's safety and security. Personal protection rituals and practices in Satanic practice are designed to create a shield of energy and intention around oneself, deflecting negativity and harm, and empowering practitioners to assert their autonomy and navigate life's challenges with confidence and resilience.

Personal protection rituals may involve acts of visualization, where practitioners imagine themselves surrounded by a shield of protective energy or invoke protective symbols or entities to ward off negative influences. These rituals are often accompanied by affirmations or intentions to assert one's boundaries, defend against external threats, and cultivate a sense of inner strength and resilience. By embracing personal protection rituals, practitioners empower themselves to take control of their environment, assert their autonomy, and create a safe and supportive space in which to thrive.

**Understanding Empowerment:**

Empowerment in Satanic philosophy involves recognizing and embracing one's innate power and potential and using it to create a life that aligns with one's deepest desires and aspirations. It is about taking ownership of one's life and choices and refusing to be defined or limited by external expectations or constraints. Empowerment rituals and practices in Satanic practice are designed to cultivate a sense of self-confidence, agency, and resilience, empowering practitioners to pursue their goals and dreams with courage and conviction.

Empowerment rituals may involve acts of self-affirmation, where practitioners vocalize their strengths, talents, and abilities or visualize themselves as powerful and unstoppable beings capable of overcoming any obstacle. These rituals are often accompanied by affirmations or intentions to embrace one's power, overcome obstacles, and manifest one's desires and aspirations. By embracing empowerment rituals, practitioners empower themselves to take control of their lives, pursue their goals with confidence and determination, and create a reality that reflects their deepest values and aspirations.

**Methods and Practices:**

Rituals for personal protection, empowerment, and defense in Satanic practice may take various forms, from simple acts of visualization and affirmation to more elaborate ceremonies and rites. The key is to choose methods and practices that resonate with the practitioner's intentions and goals and align with the principles of Satanic philosophy.

**Some common methods and practices of rituals for personal protection, empowerment, and defense include:**

Visualization techniques, where practitioners imagine themselves surrounded by a shield of protective energy or visualize themselves as powerful and unstoppable beings capable of overcoming any obstacle.

Affirmations and intentions, where practitioners vocalize their intentions to assert their boundaries, defend against external threats, and cultivate a sense of inner strength and resilience.

Ritualized ceremonies and rites, where practitioners engage in structured rituals and ceremonies to mark significant transitions, such as the initiation of a new phase of personal development or the pursuit of a specific goal or aspiration.

In conclusion, rituals for personal protection, empowerment, and defense are essential practices within Satanic philosophy, aimed at safeguarding practitioners' well-being, asserting their autonomy, and cultivating inner strength and resilience. Through rituals and practices of personal protection, empowerment, and defense, practitioners empower themselves to navigate life's challenges with confidence and determination and create a reality that reflects their deepest values and aspirations. By embracing these rituals, practitioners deepen their connection to Satanic philosophy and cultivate the inner strength and resilience needed to thrive in an often challenging world.

## Techniques for Warding Off Negative Influences and Energies

Warding off negative influences and energies is an essential aspect of Satanic practice, aimed at protecting practitioners' well-being, maintaining a positive mindset, and fostering a sense of empowerment and resilience. In this chapter, we explore various techniques for warding off negative influences and energies within the framework of Satanic philosophy. These techniques are designed to create a shield of energy and intention around practitioners, deflecting negativity, and empowering them to navigate life's challenges with confidence and resilience. Through an exploration of techniques for warding off negative influences and energies, we aim to unravel the methods and practices that enable practitioners to maintain their mental and emotional well-being and thrive in the face of adversity.

**Understanding Negative Influences and Energies:**

Negative influences and energies can come in various forms, including toxic relationships, harmful thoughts, and external stressors that undermine practitioners' well-being and hinder their personal growth and development. In Satanic philosophy, negative influences and energies are seen as obstacles to be overcome, rather than accepted or tolerated. Practitioners are encouraged to take proactive steps to protect themselves from these influences and maintain a positive and empowered mindset.

**Techniques for Warding Off Negative Influences and Energies:**

**Visualization Techniques:** Visualization is a powerful tool for warding off negative influences and energies. Practitioners can imagine themselves surrounded by a shield of protective energy, deflecting negativity and harm. Visualization can also involve envisioning a bright light or force field around oneself, repelling negative influences and creating a barrier of protection.

**Energy Clearing Practices:** Energy clearing practices involve releasing negative energy and cleansing one's aura or energy field. Techniques such as smudging with sage or other herbs, using crystals for protection, or taking a ritual bath with salt or essential oils can help to clear away negative influences and restore balance and harmony.

**Setting Boundaries:** Setting clear and firm boundaries is essential for warding off negative influences and protecting one's well-being. Practitioners are encouraged to assert their boundaries and say no to anything that compromises their values or makes them feel uncomfortable. This may involve limiting contact with toxic individuals, avoiding negative environments, or speaking up for oneself in challenging situations.

**Mindfulness and Meditation:** Mindfulness and meditation practices can help practitioners cultivate inner peace and resilience in the face of negativity. By focusing on the present moment and observing their thoughts and emotions without judgment, practitioners can develop greater awareness and control over their mental and emotional state, reducing the impact of negative influences and energies.

**Positive Affirmations and Intentions:** Positive affirmations and intentions are powerful tools for warding off negative influences and cultivating a positive mindset. Practitioners can use affirmations to reinforce their strengths, talents, and abilities, and to counteract negative self-talk or limiting beliefs. Setting positive intentions for each day or visualizing positive outcomes can also help practitioners maintain a positive and empowered mindset.

In conclusion, techniques for warding off negative influences and energies are essential practices within Satanic philosophy, aimed at protecting practitioners' well-being, maintaining a positive mindset, and fostering a sense of empowerment and resilience. Through visualization, energy clearing practices, boundary setting, mindfulness, and positive affirmations, practitioners can create a shield of energy and intention around themselves, deflecting negativity, and empowering themselves to navigate life's challenges with confidence and resilience. By embracing these techniques, practitioners deepen their connection to Satanic philosophy and cultivate the inner strength and resilience needed to thrive in an often challenging world.

## Advocacy, Activism, and Social Change

Advocacy, activism, and social change are integral aspects of Satanic philosophy, emphasizing the importance of challenging injustice, promoting individual rights, and advocating for a more equitable and compassionate society. In this chapter, we explore the role of advocacy, activism, and social change within the framework of Satanic practice. These principles are rooted in the Satanic tenets of compassion, empathy, and individualism, and guide practitioners in their efforts to effect positive change in the world. Through an exploration of advocacy, activism, and social change, we aim to unravel the methods and practices that enable practitioners to advocate for their beliefs, challenge social norms, and create a more just and inclusive society.

**Understanding Advocacy, Activism, and Social Change:**

Advocacy involves speaking out on behalf of oneself or others, promoting awareness of issues, and advocating for change. Activism, on the other hand, involves taking action to effect change, whether through protests, petitions, or other forms of direct action. Social change refers to the broader transformation of society's norms, values, and institutions to create a more equitable and just world. Together, advocacy, activism, and social change form the foundation of Satanic efforts to challenge injustice, promote individual rights, and create a more compassionate and inclusive society.

### The Role of Advocacy, Activism, and Social Change in Satanic Practice:

Advocacy, activism, and social change are central to Satanic practice, as they align with the core principles of compassion, empathy, and individualism. Satanic philosophy emphasizes the importance of standing up for one's beliefs, advocating for individual rights, and challenging authority and injustice. Practitioners are encouraged to use their voices and their actions to effect positive change in the world and to promote a society that respects and values diversity, equality, and human rights.

### Methods and Practices:

There are many ways that practitioners can engage in advocacy, activism, and social change within the framework of Satanic practice. Some common methods and practices include:

**Education and Awareness:** Practitioners can educate themselves and others about social justice issues, human rights, and the importance of advocacy and activism. This may involve reading books, attending workshops, or engaging in discussions with others to raise awareness and promote understanding of these issues.

**Direct Action:** Direct action involves taking tangible steps to effect change, such as participating in protests, marches, or demonstrations, signing petitions, or contacting elected officials to voice concerns and advocate for policy changes.

**Community Engagement:** Practitioners can get involved in their communities by volunteering with local organizations, supporting grassroots movements, or organizing events and activities to promote social justice and equality.

**Artistic Expression:** Artistic expression can be a powerful tool for advocacy and activism, allowing practitioners to convey messages and provoke thought through visual art, music, literature, or performance.

**Legal Advocacy:** Practitioners can support legal efforts to promote social justice and human rights by volunteering with legal aid organizations, advocating for policy changes, or supporting individuals who have been unjustly targeted or marginalized.

In conclusion, advocacy, activism, and social change are integral aspects of Satanic practice, reflecting the core principles of compassion, empathy, and individualism. Through advocacy, activism, and social change, practitioners can challenge injustice, promote individual rights, and create a more equitable and compassionate society. By engaging in education and awareness, direct action, community engagement, artistic expression, and legal advocacy, practitioners empower themselves to effect positive change in the world and to promote a society that respects and values diversity, equality, and human rights.

Through an exploration of advocacy, activism, and social change, practitioners deepen their connection to Satanic philosophy and contribute to the ongoing effort to create a more just and inclusive world.

## The Role of Rituals in Promoting Satanic Values and Challenging Social Norms

Rituals play a significant role in Satanic practice, serving as powerful tools for promoting Satanic values and challenging social norms. In this chapter, we explore the importance of rituals within the framework of Satanic philosophy. Rituals are not only symbolic acts of worship or devotion but also opportunities for practitioners to express their beliefs, assert their individuality, and challenge societal conventions. Through an exploration of the role of rituals in promoting Satanic values and challenging social norms, we aim to unravel the methods and practices that enable practitioners to embody their beliefs and effect change in the world.

**Rituals as Expressions of Satanic Values:**

Rituals in Satanic practice serve as expressions of Satanic values, such as individualism, rationalism, and personal empowerment. These values are central to Satanic philosophy and are reflected in the themes, symbols, and actions of Satanic rituals. By engaging in rituals that affirm these values, practitioners reinforce their commitment to Satanic principles and assert their autonomy and sovereignty.

For example, rituals focused on personal empowerment may involve acts of visualization, affirmation, or symbolic gestures that reinforce practitioners' sense of self-worth, strength, and resilience. Similarly, rituals that celebrate individuality may involve creative expression, artistic performance, or group activities that highlight the diversity and uniqueness of each practitioner.

**Challenging Social Norms:**

In addition to promoting Satanic values, rituals in Satanic practice also serve as a means of challenging social norms and conventions. Satanic rituals often involve acts or symbols that are deliberately provocative or controversial, challenging societal taboos and expectations and encouraging practitioners to think critically about the world around them.

For example, rituals that incorporate themes of sexuality, taboo, or transgression may challenge societal attitudes towards these topics and promote a more open and inclusive perspective. Similarly, rituals that celebrate non-traditional forms of family, community, or spirituality may challenge traditional notions of what constitutes a "normal" or "acceptable" way of life.

**Methods and Practices:**

There are many ways that rituals in Satanic practice can promote Satanic values and challenge social norms. Some common methods and practices include:

**Symbolic Acts:** Rituals often involve symbolic acts or gestures that represent Satanic values and beliefs. These acts may include gestures of defiance, such as the raising of the fist or the breaking of chains, or acts of celebration, such as the lighting of candles or the sharing of food and drink.

**Visual Imagery:** Visual imagery plays a powerful role in Satanic rituals, with symbols and icons representing key aspects of Satanic philosophy. Practitioners may use imagery such as the Sigil of Baphomet, the inverted pentagram, or other Satanic symbols to evoke feelings of empowerment, liberation, and defiance.

**Group Dynamics:** Group rituals can be particularly effective in promoting Satanic values and challenging social norms. By coming together as a community, practitioners reinforce their shared commitment to Satanic principles and create a supportive environment in which to explore and express their beliefs.

In conclusion, rituals play a vital role in Satanic practice, serving as powerful tools for promoting Satanic values and challenging social norms. Through rituals that celebrate individualism, empowerment, and non-conformity, practitioners reaffirm their commitment to Satanic philosophy and assert their autonomy and sovereignty. By engaging in rituals that provoke thought, inspire creativity, and encourage critical reflection, practitioners challenge societal taboos and expectations and promote a more inclusive and compassionate world. Through an exploration of the role of rituals in promoting Satanic values and challenging social norms, practitioners deepen their connection to Satanic philosophy and contribute to the ongoing effort to create a world that embraces diversity, equality, and individual freedom.

# Satanic Rituals for Advocacy, Activism, and Fighting Injustice

Satanic rituals are not only expressions of personal beliefs and values but also powerful tools for advocacy, activism, and fighting injustice. In this chapter, we delve into the significance of Satanic rituals in promoting social change and challenging systemic injustices. Satanic philosophy encourages practitioners to actively engage in advocacy and activism, using rituals as a means to amplify their voices, raise awareness, and effect positive change in the world. Through an exploration of Satanic rituals for advocacy, activism, and fighting injustice, we aim to unravel the methods and practices that enable practitioners to stand up against oppression, promote equality, and create a more just and compassionate society.

**Rituals as Acts of Resistance:**

Satanic rituals can serve as acts of resistance against oppressive systems and structures, challenging societal norms and advocating for marginalized communities. These rituals often incorporate themes of empowerment, liberation, and defiance, empowering practitioners to confront injustice and fight for equality.

For example, rituals may involve symbolic acts of rebellion, such as the breaking of chains or the tearing down of barriers, to represent the dismantling of oppressive systems. Visual imagery, such as the use of Satanic symbols or iconography, can also serve as a powerful means of resistance, challenging dominant narratives and asserting the autonomy and sovereignty of practitioners.

**Empowerment Rituals for Activism:**

Empowerment rituals are particularly effective in preparing practitioners for activism and advocacy work, providing them with the strength, resilience, and determination needed to confront injustice and effect change. These rituals may involve acts of visualization, affirmation, or meditation, empowering practitioners to tap into their inner strength and harness their energy for positive action.

For example, rituals may include visualizations of practitioners surrounded by a shield of protective energy, deflecting negativity and harm as they engage in activism and advocacy work. Affirmations and intentions may reinforce practitioners' commitment to fighting injustice and promoting equality, providing them with the mental and emotional fortitude needed to persevere in the face of adversity.

**Group Rituals for Collective Action:**

Group rituals play a crucial role in fostering collective action and solidarity among Satanic practitioners, providing them with a sense of community and support as they engage in advocacy and activism work. By coming together as a community, practitioners amplify their voices, share resources, and strengthen their resolve to effect positive change in the world.

Group rituals may involve collective acts of empowerment, such as group meditations or energy-raising exercises, to build solidarity and unity among practitioners. They may also include rituals that honor the contributions of activists and advocates who have fought for social justice throughout history, inspiring practitioners to continue their work and carry on their legacy.

In conclusion, Satanic rituals are powerful tools for advocacy, activism, and fighting injustice, empowering practitioners to confront oppression and effect positive change in the world. Through rituals that embody themes of resistance, empowerment, and collective action, practitioners challenge societal norms, advocate for marginalized communities, and promote equality and justice for all. By harnessing the transformative power of ritual, Satanic practitioners deepen their commitment to social change and contribute to the ongoing effort to create a more just and compassionate society.

## Ethics, Respect, and Non-Violence

Ethics, respect, and non-violence are foundational principles within Satanic philosophy, guiding practitioners in their interactions with others and their approach to the world. In this chapter, we explore the importance of ethics, respect, and non-violence within the framework of Satanic practice. These principles reflect the core values of compassion, empathy, and individual autonomy, and serve as guiding principles for practitioners as they navigate their lives and engage with the world around them. Through an exploration of ethics, respect, and non-violence, we aim to unravel the methods and practices that enable practitioners to embody these principles and contribute to a more harmonious and compassionate society.

**Ethical Considerations in Satanic Practice:**

Ethics are central to Satanic philosophy, emphasizing the importance of personal responsibility, integrity, and accountability. Satanic ethics are rooted in the principle of individual autonomy, affirming each person's right to make their own choices and live according to their own values and beliefs. Practitioners are encouraged to act with honesty, integrity, and compassion, and to consider the consequences of their actions on themselves and others.

**Respect for Others:**

Respect for others is a fundamental aspect of Satanic practice, recognizing the inherent worth and dignity of every individual, regardless of their beliefs, background, or identity. Satanic philosophy promotes tolerance, empathy, and understanding, encouraging practitioners to treat others with kindness, compassion, and respect. Practitioners are encouraged to listen to others with an open mind, to seek to understand different perspectives, and to engage in constructive dialogue and debate.

**Non-Violence as a Core Principle:**

Non-violence is a core principle within Satanic philosophy, reflecting the belief that violence and aggression are antithetical to personal growth, empowerment, and social progress. Satanic philosophy promotes peaceful conflict resolution, emphasizing the importance of dialogue, negotiation, and compromise in resolving differences and addressing conflict. Practitioners are encouraged to reject violence in all its forms and to seek non-violent solutions to conflicts and disagreements.

**Methods and Practices:**

There are many ways that practitioners can embody ethics, respect, and non-violence in their daily lives and interactions. Some common methods and practices include:

**Practicing Empathy:** Practitioners can cultivate empathy by putting themselves in others' shoes and seeking to understand their perspectives, feelings, and experiences. Empathy promotes compassion, understanding, and connection, fostering positive relationships and mutual respect.

**Acting with Integrity:** Practitioners can demonstrate integrity by acting in accordance with their values and principles, even when faced with temptation or pressure to compromise. Integrity builds trust and credibility, both within the Satanic community and in society at large.

**Respecting Boundaries:** Practitioners can show respect for others by honoring their boundaries, both physical and emotional. Respecting boundaries promotes trust, safety, and mutual respect in relationships, fostering healthy and positive interactions.

**Promoting Non-Violence:** Practitioners can promote non-violence by actively opposing violence and aggression in all its forms, both in their personal lives and in society. This may involve speaking out against injustice, supporting peaceful protests and demonstrations, and advocating for non-violent conflict resolution.

In conclusion, ethics, respect, and non-violence are foundational principles within Satanic philosophy, guiding practitioners in their interactions with others and their approach to the world. By embodying these principles in their daily lives and interactions, practitioners contribute to a more harmonious and compassionate society, where individuals are treated with dignity, compassion, and respect. Through an exploration of ethics, respect, and non-violence, practitioners deepen their commitment to Satanic philosophy and foster positive relationships and communities based on empathy, understanding, and mutual respect.

## The Ethical Framework of Contemporary Satanism

Contemporary Satanism encompasses a diverse range of beliefs and practices, but at its core lies an ethical framework that guides practitioners in their interactions with others and their approach to the world. In this chapter, we delve into the ethical principles that underpin contemporary Satanism, exploring how they shape the beliefs and actions of practitioners. These ethical principles reflect values such as individual autonomy, compassion, and personal responsibility, and serve as a foundation for Satanic philosophy. Through an exploration of the ethical framework of contemporary Satanism, we aim to unravel the methods and practices that enable practitioners to embody these principles and contribute to a more just and compassionate society.

**Individual Autonomy and Personal Responsibility:**

At the heart of contemporary Satanism is the principle of individual autonomy, which asserts each person's right to make their own choices and live according to their own values and beliefs. Practitioners are encouraged to take responsibility for their actions and decisions, recognizing that they alone are responsible for the consequences of their choices. This emphasis on personal responsibility fosters accountability and integrity, empowering practitioners to navigate their lives with clarity and purpose.

**Compassion and Empathy:**

Contemporary Satanism also emphasizes the importance of compassion and empathy, encouraging practitioners to treat others with kindness, understanding, and respect. Practitioners are encouraged to cultivate empathy by putting themselves in others' shoes and seeking to understand their perspectives, feelings, and experiences. Compassion promotes solidarity, cooperation, and mutual support, fostering positive relationships and communities based on empathy and understanding.

**Non-Violence and Peaceful Conflict Resolution:**

Non-violence is a core principle within contemporary Satanism, reflecting the belief that violence and aggression are antithetical to personal growth, empowerment, and social progress. Practitioners are encouraged to reject violence in all its forms and to seek non-violent solutions to conflicts and disagreements. This may involve promoting dialogue, negotiation, and compromise as means of resolving differences and addressing conflict. By embracing non-violence, practitioners contribute to a culture of peace, tolerance, and respect for human rights.

**Ethical Considerations in Rituals and Practices:**

Ethical considerations also play a significant role in the rituals and practices of contemporary Satanism. Practitioners are encouraged to conduct themselves with integrity and respect in their interactions with others, both within and outside of ritual contexts. Rituals are conducted with mindfulness and intention, with practitioners taking care to ensure that their actions do not cause harm or offense to others. Ethical considerations also inform practitioners' choices regarding the use of symbols, imagery, and language in rituals, with practitioners seeking to uphold principles of inclusivity, diversity, and respect.

In conclusion, the ethical framework of contemporary Satanism is grounded in principles of individual autonomy, compassion, and non-violence. Practitioners are encouraged to take responsibility for their actions, treat others with kindness and respect, and seek non-violent solutions to conflicts and disagreements. By embodying these principles in their daily lives and interactions, practitioners contribute to a more just, compassionate, and harmonious society. Through an exploration of the ethical framework of contemporary Satanism, practitioners deepen their commitment to Satanic philosophy and foster positive relationships and communities based on empathy, understanding, and mutual respect.

## Emphasizing Respect for Others and Non-Violence in Satanic Practice

Respect for others and non-violence are core principles within Satanic practice, reflecting the values of compassion, empathy, and individual autonomy. In this chapter, we delve into the importance of emphasizing respect for others and non-violence in Satanic practice. These principles guide practitioners in their interactions with others and their approach to conflict resolution, fostering a culture of empathy, understanding, and mutual respect. Through an exploration of respect for others and non-violence in Satanic practice, we aim to unravel the methods and practices that enable practitioners to embody these principles and contribute to a more harmonious and compassionate society.

**Respect for Others:**

Respect for others is a fundamental aspect of Satanic practice, recognizing the inherent worth and dignity of every individual, regardless of their beliefs, background, or identity. Satanic philosophy promotes tolerance, empathy, and understanding, encouraging practitioners to treat others with kindness, compassion, and respect. Practitioners are encouraged to listen to others with an open mind, to seek to understand different perspectives, and to engage in constructive dialogue and debate.

**Non-Violence as a Core Principle:**

Non-violence is a core principle within Satanic philosophy, reflecting the belief that violence and aggression are antithetical to personal growth, empowerment, and social progress. Satanic philosophy promotes peaceful conflict resolution, emphasizing the importance of dialogue, negotiation, and compromise in resolving differences and addressing conflict. Practitioners are encouraged to reject violence in all its forms and to seek non-violent solutions to conflicts and disagreements.

**Methods and Practices:**

There are many ways that practitioners can emphasize respect for others and non-violence in their daily lives and interactions. Some common methods and practices include:

**Cultivating Empathy:** Practitioners can cultivate empathy by putting themselves in others' shoes and seeking to understand their perspectives, feelings, and experiences. Empathy promotes compassion, understanding, and connection, fostering positive relationships and mutual respect.

**Acting with Integrity:** Practitioners can demonstrate integrity by acting in accordance with their values and principles, even when faced with temptation or pressure to compromise. Integrity builds trust and credibility, both within the Satanic community and in society at large.

**Respecting Boundaries:** Practitioners can show respect for others by honoring their boundaries, both physical and emotional. Respecting boundaries promotes trust, safety, and mutual respect in relationships, fostering healthy and positive interactions.

**Promoting Non-Violence:** Practitioners can promote non-violence by actively opposing violence and aggression in all its forms, both in their personal lives and in society. This may involve speaking out against injustice, supporting peaceful protests and demonstrations, and advocating for non-violent conflict resolution.

In conclusion, emphasizing respect for others and non-violence is essential in Satanic practice, fostering a culture of empathy, understanding, and mutual respect. Through practices that cultivate empathy, integrity, and respect for boundaries, practitioners contribute to a more harmonious and compassionate society, where individuals are treated with dignity, compassion, and respect. By rejecting violence and promoting non-violent solutions to conflicts and disagreements, practitioners uphold the core principles of Satanic philosophy and contribute to a culture of peace, tolerance, and respect for human rights. Through an exploration of respect for others and non-violence in Satanic practice, practitioners deepen their commitment to Satanic philosophy and foster positive relationships and communities based on empathy, understanding, and mutual respect.

## Reflecting on the Diversity and Complexity of Satanic Rituals and Practices

Satanic rituals and practices encompass a diverse array of beliefs, traditions, and interpretations, reflecting the complexity and richness of Satanic philosophy. In this chapter, we explore the diversity and complexity of Satanic rituals and practices, examining the various forms they take and the myriad ways in which they are interpreted and practiced by individuals and groups around the world. From solemn ceremonies to joyous celebrations, Satanic rituals and practices are as diverse as the practitioners who engage in them, reflecting a wide range of cultural influences, personal beliefs, and philosophical perspectives. Through an exploration of the diversity and complexity of Satanic rituals and practices, we aim to unravel the methods, meanings, and significance behind these varied expressions of Satanic philosophy.

**The Multifaceted Nature of Satanic Rituals:**

Satanic rituals are multifaceted and diverse, encompassing a wide range of practices, traditions, and beliefs. While some rituals may be solemn and ceremonial, others may be lighthearted and celebratory, reflecting the diversity of Satanic philosophy and the individual preferences and beliefs of practitioners. Satanic rituals may involve elements such as symbolism, invocation, meditation, and performance, with practitioners drawing on a variety of cultural, religious, and occult traditions to create meaningful and transformative experiences.

**Interpretations and Perspectives:**

The interpretation of Satanic rituals and practices can vary widely among practitioners, with individuals and groups bringing their own unique perspectives, beliefs, and experiences to their understanding of Satanic philosophy. Some practitioners may view rituals as symbolic acts of worship or devotion, while others may see them as opportunities for personal growth, empowerment, and self-expression. Still, others may approach rituals from a more philosophical or psychological perspective, viewing them as tools for exploring the depths of the human psyche and unlocking hidden potentials.

**Cultural Influences and Traditions:**

Satanic rituals and practices are often influenced by a variety of cultural, religious, and occult traditions, reflecting the diverse backgrounds and experiences of practitioners. From ancient pagan rituals to modern occult practices, Satanic rituals may draw on a wide range of sources and influences, incorporating elements such as symbolism, mythology, and ritualistic symbolism. These cultural influences and traditions add depth and richness to Satanic rituals, allowing practitioners to connect with a broader array of spiritual and philosophical concepts.

**Personalization and Innovation:**

One of the defining features of Satanic rituals and practices is their emphasis on individualism and personal autonomy, allowing practitioners to personalize and innovate their rituals to suit their own beliefs, preferences, and needs. Satanic rituals may be adapted and modified over time, with practitioners incorporating new elements, symbols, and practices into their rituals to reflect their evolving understanding of Satanic philosophy. This spirit of personalization and innovation ensures that Satanic rituals remain vibrant, dynamic, and relevant to practitioners in a constantly changing world.

In conclusion, Satanic rituals and practices are diverse, complex, and multifaceted, reflecting the richness and diversity of Satanic philosophy. From solemn ceremonies to joyous celebrations, Satanic rituals encompass a wide range of beliefs, traditions, and interpretations, allowing practitioners to explore and express their beliefs in meaningful and transformative ways. By embracing diversity and complexity in Satanic rituals and practices, practitioners deepen their understanding of Satanic philosophy and create meaningful and authentic spiritual experiences that resonate with their individual beliefs, values, and aspirations. Through an exploration of the diversity and complexity of Satanic rituals and practices, practitioners celebrate the richness and diversity of Satanic philosophy and affirm their commitment to personal autonomy, individualism, and self-expression.

# Looking Ahead: The Future of Satanism in a Changing World

As we stand on the threshold of a new era, the future of Satanism is being shaped by a rapidly changing world, marked by shifting cultural, social, and technological landscapes. In this very expanded chapter, we explore the evolving nature of Satanism and the challenges and opportunities that lie ahead for practitioners in the years to come. From the impact of globalization and digital technology to the emergence of new social movements and cultural trends, the future of Satanism promises to be both dynamic and transformative. Through an in-depth exploration of the future of Satanism, we aim to unravel the key trends, developments, and possibilities that will shape the evolution of Satanic philosophy and practice in the years ahead.

**Globalization and Cultural Exchange:**

One of the most significant trends shaping the future of Satanism is the ongoing process of globalization, which has facilitated increased cultural exchange and interaction among people from diverse backgrounds and traditions. As Satanic philosophy continues to spread and evolve around the world, practitioners are increasingly drawing on a wide range of cultural, religious, and philosophical influences to inform their beliefs and practices. This globalization of Satanism has the potential to enrich and diversify Satanic philosophy, as practitioners draw inspiration from a broader array of cultural traditions and perspectives.

**Digital Technology and Online Communities:**

The rise of digital technology and online communities has transformed the way in which Satanic philosophy is shared, discussed, and practiced. Social media platforms, online forums, and digital publications have provided practitioners with new avenues for connecting with like-minded individuals, sharing ideas and experiences, and organizing events and activities. The internet has also facilitated the dissemination of Satanic literature, music, and artwork, allowing practitioners to access a wealth of resources and information from around the world. As digital technology continues to evolve, the role of online communities in shaping the future of Satanism is likely to grow, providing practitioners with new opportunities for collaboration, education, and activism.

**Social Movements and Activism:**

Satanism has long been associated with countercultural movements and activism, challenging traditional norms and values and advocating for individual autonomy and freedom of expression. In the future, Satanic philosophy is likely to continue to intersect with social movements and activism, as practitioners engage with issues such as social justice, environmentalism, and human rights. From organizing protests and demonstrations to supporting grassroots initiatives and advocacy campaigns, practitioners are increasingly using Satanic philosophy as a platform for promoting positive social change and challenging systemic injustices.

**Cultural Trends and Expressions:**

As society evolves, so too does the cultural landscape in which Satanic philosophy is situated. From literature and film to music and art, Satanic themes and imagery continue to permeate popular culture, reflecting broader cultural trends and expressions. In the future, Satanic philosophy is likely to continue to influence and be influenced by these cultural trends, as practitioners engage with and respond to the changing cultural landscape. Whether through the creation of Satanic-themed artwork, literature, or music, practitioners will continue to express and explore Satanic philosophy in diverse and innovative ways, shaping the future of Satanism as a vibrant and dynamic cultural phenomenon.

In conclusion, the future of Satanism promises to be both dynamic and transformative, shaped by a range of cultural, social, and technological trends and developments. From the impact of globalization and digital technology to the emergence of new social movements and cultural expressions, Satanic philosophy is poised to evolve and adapt in response to the changing world around us. As practitioners navigate the challenges and opportunities of the future, they will continue to uphold the core principles of Satanic philosophy, promoting individual autonomy, personal responsibility, and compassion in an ever-changing world. Through an exploration of the future of Satanism, practitioners reaffirm their commitment to Satanic philosophy and embrace the possibilities of a future that is both challenging and full of potential.

Satanists have an equivalent to the 10 commandments or the 7 deadly sins.

## The Satanic Temple has 7 Fundamental Tenets:

One should strive to act with compassion and empathy toward all creatures in accordance with reason

The struggle for justice is an ongoing and necessary pursuit that should prevail over laws and institutions.

One's body is inviolable, subject to one's own will alone.

The freedoms of others should be respected, including the freedom to offend. To willfully and unjustly encroach upon the freedoms of another is to forgo one's own.

Beliefs should conform to one's best scientific understanding of the world. One should take care never to distort scientific facts to fit one's beliefs.

People are fallible. If one makes a mistake, one should do one's best to rectify it and resolve any harm that might have been caused.

Every tenet is a guiding principle designed to inspire nobility in action and thought. The spirit of compassion, wisdom, and justice should always prevail over the written or spoken word.

## The Church of Satan has the 9 Satanic Statements:

- Satan represents indulgence instead of abstinence!
- Satan represents vital existence instead of spiritual pipe dreams!
- Satan represents undefiled wisdom instead of hypocritical self-deceit!
- Satan represents kindness to those who deserve it instead of love wasted on ingrates!
- Satan represents vengeance instead of turning the other cheek!
- Satan represents responsibility to the responsible instead of concern for psychic vampires!
- Satan represents man as just another animal, sometimes better, more often worse than those that walk on all-fours, who, because of his "divine spiritual and intellectual development," has become the most vicious animal of all!

- Satan represents all of the so-called sins, as they all lead to physical, mental, or emotional gratification!
- Satan has been the best friend the Church has ever had, as He has kept it in business all these years!

## 11 Rules of the Earth:

- Do not give opinions or advice unless you are asked.
- Do not tell your troubles to others unless you are sure they want to hear them.
- When in another's lair, show him respect or else do not go there.
- If a guest in your lair annoys you, treat him cruelly and without mercy.
- Do not make sexual advances unless you are given the mating signal.
- Do not take that which does not belong to you unless it is a burden to the other person and he cries out to be relieved.
- Acknowledge the power of magic if you have employed it successfully to obtain your desires. If you deny the power of magic after having called upon it with success, you will lose all you have obtained.
- Do not complain about anything to which you need not subject yourself.
- Do not harm little children.
- Do not kill non-human animals unless you are attacked or for your food.
- When walking in open territory, bother no one. If someone bothers you, ask him to stop. If he does not stop, destroy him.

## and 9 Satanic Sins:

- Stupidity
- Pretentiousness
- Solipsism
- Self-deceit
- Herd conformity
- Lack of perspective
- Forgetfulness of past orthodoxies
- Counterproductive pride
- Lack of aesthetics

There are many more lesser known satanic organizations with their own guiding principles but the two most famous organizations are The Satanic Temple and the Church of Satan.

# Epilogue

In the fading twilight of a tumultuous journey into the dark recesses of human fascination, our exploration of "The Mysteries of Satanic Rituals and Forbidden Rites" finds its conclusion. As the pages turn and the whispers of ancient secrets settle, we are left to ponder the boundaries between fascination and fear, curiosity and caution.

Yet, amid the shadows cast by the rituals described within, a glimmer of enlightenment emerges. For in our quest to understand the forbidden, we have uncovered not only the depths of human darkness but also the resilience of the human spirit.

As the final words of the tome fade into memory, let us carry forward the wisdom gained from our exploration, recognizing that true power lies not in the shadows but in the light of understanding. And may we, armed with knowledge and tempered by wisdom, navigate the labyrinth of existence with courage and compassion, ever mindful of the mysteries that dwell within and without.

Printed in Great Britain
by Amazon

cbac5771-5cb6-4fff-bec6-4cc01ff89de2R02